In Performance

MW00355468

EDITED BY
CAROL MARTIN

In Performance is a book series devoted to national and global theater of the twenty-first century. Scholarly essays providing the theatrical, cultural, and political contexts for the plays and performance texts introduce each volume. The texts are written both by established and emerging writers, translated by accomplished translators and aimed at people who want to put new works on stage, read diverse dramatic and performance literature, and study diverse theater practices, contexts, and histories in light of globalization.

In Performance has been supported by translation and editing grants from the following organizations:

The Book Institute, Krakow
TEDA Project, Istanbul
The Memorial Fund for Jewish Culture, New York
Polish Cultural Institute, New York
Zbigniew Raszewski Theatrical Institute, Warsaw
Adam Mickiewicz Institute, Warsaw
Goethe-Institut, New York
Austrian Cultural Forum, New York

NOTHING TO DO WITH LOVE

and Other Plays

SANTIAGO LOZA

EDITED BY
Samuel Buggeln and Noe Montez

TRANSLATED BY
Samuel Buggeln and Ariel Gurevich

LONDON NEW YORK CALCUTTA

Seagull Books, 2021

All plays © Santiago Loza
Foreword © Samuel Buggeln, 2021
Introduction © Noe Montez, 2021
Translations © Samuel Buggeln and Ariel Gurevich, 2021
Photographs © Individual photographers, 2021
This compilation © Seagull Books, 2021

ISBN 978 0 8574 2 897 4

British Library Cataloging-in-Publication Data
A catalog record for this book is available from the British Library

Book designed by Bishan Samaddar, Seagull Books, Calcutta, India
Printed and bound by Hyam Enterprises, Calcutta, India

CONTENTS

Samuel Buggeln

This book began with a Craigslist ad. Just over six years ago as I write this foreword, my partner and I had embarked on a six-month sabbatical to Buenos Aires. Nick was writing a book, and I, burning out on a New York–based freelance directing career, was investigating the action in what I had heard was one of the most extraordinary theater cities in the world. I didn't know what I needed, aside from change and new information, but we reasoned that Buenos Aires would provide both.

In that fast-talking town, I soon realized my Spanish needed work, and one Craigslist ad seemed promising. Improve your Spanish, one-on-one or in small groups, through an engagement with Argentine "objetos culturales": films, plays, fiction. I emailed that day, and the young man who replied was able to meet on the next. At the session, my friendly tutor ascertained that I was a theater director (something I suspect he had already done by clicking the website in my email signature), and asked if I was interested in Buenos Aires theater. When I said I was, he began to list playwrights of interest on a sheet of paper, noting those more and less celebrated, and especially who had studied under whom. In Argentina, rather than pursuing MFAs, aspiring playwrights take master classes with more senior writers, a tradition that has now been going on long enough that distinct lineages can be traced.

I looked at the piece of paper covered in names of Argentine play-wrights, including several from previous generations, arranged in ladders and networks of aesthetic influence. You know a lot about Argentine the-ater, I said. Yes, he said. I'm lucky to have stumbled on you through Craigslist, I said. Yes, he said.

At the center of the page, probably underlined, was the name Santiago Loza. Then as now, Loza was probably the most produced playwright in town. So I would likely have come to know his work even if Ariel, my new tutor, had not been a friend and colleague of his.

During that extraordinary six months in Buenos Aires, I saw some fifty shows, often guided by Ariel's recommendations. These included productions of Loza's *La mujer puerca* (*The Saint*), *El mal de la montaña* (*Altitude Sickness*), and of course *Nada del amor me produce envidia* (*Nothing to Do with Love [Makes Me Envious]*), all of which plays appear in this volume.

I imagine many Anglo-world theater directors will be familiar with this phenomenon: while watching a production, one automatically mentally extracts the text, imagining it independent of the current performance, and idly visualizing one's own production of the play. (Sometimes these imaginary productions are exciting; often they don't add up to much.) In Buenos Aires, I found myself doing that, more or less as usual, but with an added layer of complexity: as I visualized a play in my own production, by force of habit I also imagined it in English. Often this exercise produced a clumsy or fuzzy picture: for a wide range of reasons, many plays that are excellent in Buenos Aires didn't feel like they would resonate in English and/or in North America. But sometimes they sang. I didn't arrive planning to make these assessments; indeed, as I made them, they were not even fully conscious. But toward the end of my time in Argentina, I was in possession of a short list of theater writers that I was quite obsessed with translating into English.

Loza was not the first writer I approached Ariel, by now a good friend, about co-translating. Instead, he and I co-translated a typically wild and woolly play by the extraordinary Argentine writer, actor, and director, Rafael Spregelburd.[1]

It is hard to think of two more different theater writers than Loza and Spregelburd. The latter writes dizzyingly complex plays full of intellectual

---

1 That translation, *Why Does Everything* [*Todo*] appears in *The Mercurian* 7(2) (Fall 2018). Available at: https://the-mercurian.com/2018/11/08/why-does-everything/ (last accessed on October 19, 2021).

and political provocation, and is a star of the European contemporary theater circuit, in particular Berlin's Schaubühne. By contrast, I think of Loza
as "the people's playwright," creating engaging monologues full of deep
poetry and close psychological observation—works that could run in
Buenos Aires for years on end, to ecstatic reviews, the public returning
season after season to theaters small and large to be drawn into his characters' moving and deeply personal stories.

You can guess the next step. It was such a pleasure to collaborate with
Ariel on Sprebelburd's text that I persuaded him to work with me on Loza's
writing: the plays you are about to read.

I had translated solo before, from French, but the process of co-
translation was unusually thought-provoking. Here, one of us had a deep
knowledge of the functioning of the source language and plays; the other
a similar knowledge of effective theater texts in English. And the conversations between these two bodies of knowledge, rather than happening
inside one brain, took place aloud, in real time, at first in Buenos Aires
cafes and later on computer screens. This may be why the process stimu-
lated me to so much reflection on the nature of translating for the theater.
I include some of these thoughts in co-translator/co-editor's notes after
the plays. I'm grateful to Ariel for his patience in partnering with me on
this project over a half-decade, even as his own career as a playwright and
theater creator in Buenos Aires has blossomed.

*

Upon my return to the US, some colleagues and I founded the Cherry
Artists' Collective, an ensemble dedicated in part to producing works of
theater in translation. Three seasons ago, we produced Loza's *Nothing to
Do with Love* and *Winter Animals.*[2] And recently, while Loza was fortu-
itously in the US, we produced *The Saint* as part of a festival of (almost-)
solo works for women performers. The translated texts of those three plays

---

2 The year before that, the Cherry produced a play by Rafael Spregelburd: *Spam*,
translated by the invaluable scholar of Argentine theater, Jean Graham-Jones.

were enriched by the contributions of the production teams, and Ariel and I thank them for their talent and labour.[3] I am also indebted to Noe Montez, who, when this stack of playscripts wanted to become a book, agreed to join us as co-editor and introduction writer, contributing his deep knowledge and insight on Buenos Aires' theater. Carol Martin and the fine people at Seagull Books provided enthusiasm and sound advice, for which I thank them. And finally, I thank Nick Salvato, the partner I name in the first sentence, since become co-founder of a joyful theater collective, and always my greatest source of support, love, and interlocution.

January 2019

---

3 Credits for these productions appear in the Appendix.

SANTIAGO LOZA AND THE ARGENTINE THEATER
Marginalization, Resilience, and Innovation[1]

Noe Montez

Theater is deeply connected to twentieth- and twenty-first-century Argentine history and culture. Buenos Aires in particular is renowned for its theatrical activity and for being one of the most theatrically innovative cities in Latin America as well as one of the most prolific theater-producing cities in the world. Hundreds of plays and musicals are staged across the city on any given night, in venues that range from traditional proscenium houses to bars, as well as other public and private spaces. The city's production model facilitates plays that run an hour or less in length, so that active theatergoers may traverse several neighborhoods in order to see multiple productions in the same evening. Importantly, theater also thrives in several other Argentine cities, including Santa Fe, Mendoza, Tucumán, and Córdoba. These municipalities have their own theater funding mechanisms, and produce quality work by trained, high-caliber theater professionals at performance spaces that are both impressive architectural structures and equipped with extraordinary technical capabilities.

Although the lines between categories continue to blur, Buenos Aires's productions may be divided into three distinct groups: commercial theater, state-supported theater, and independent theater. Avenida Corrientes functions as the city's Broadway equivalent, hosting commercial, Spanish-language translations of hit shows from Broadway or the West End. The city's state-supported theaters program a wide variety of classics from within and beyond Argentina in addition to contemporary work from

---

1 Sections of this essay build upon work published in *Memory, Transitional Justice, and Theatre in Postdictatorship Argentina* (Carbondale, IL: Southern Illinois University Press, 2018).

some of the country's most acclaimed dramatists. Yet the most versatile and dynamic theater produced in the city comes from its "off-Corrientes" independent theater, which has produced dozens of playwrights whose work is performed nationally and at major international festivals. These productions also populate the city's Festival Internacional de Buenos Aires, which showcases artists for international programmers. The independent-theater playwrights have made a broad commitment to staging work with universal themes, aesthetic experimentation, and legibility to foreign audiences while still speaking to concerns relevant in Argentina.

Throughout the 1990s and the early years of the twenty-first century, many of the artists who rejuvenated the city's independent-theater scene were part of the generation occasionally referred to as *teatro joven*, or the young theater. They tend to work across performative boundaries, and function as actors, directors, designers, playwrights, musicians, composers, as well as producers. Several also work prolifically in television and film. These artists work across multiple companies and venues, and utilize their imagination to create work within limited budgets and in spite of socioeconomic and political challenges that continually undermine theatrical production. They display a tremendous spirit of innovation and flexibility in order to create productions that provoke both domestic and international audiences. Although many major playwrights of this period (Lola Arias, Rafael Spregelburd, Mariano Pensotti, Javier Daulte, Federico León) have received critical attention from the academic world, numerous others have not.

This anthology is devoted to the theatrical writing of Santiago Loza, one of Buenos Aires's most produced playwrights, and an author who draws upon many of the nation's twentieth- and twenty-first-century theatrical traditions to give voice to marginalized and under-represented people. In order to situate Loza's work within the context of Argentine theater history, as well as its contemporary-theater scene, I begin with an overview of the major trends in twentieth- and twenty-first-century Argentine theater before turning to Loza's career as a dramatist, the plays featured in this compilation, and an analysis of the ways in which Loza consciously places himself in conversation with Argentina's history and politics.

Through good and bad economic climates, Buenos Aires's theaters have remained resilient, evolving in style and form in order to reflect political changes and shifts in *porteño* aesthetic sensibilities. Modern Argentina emerged in the late nineteenth and early twentieth century, when an influx of European immigrants arrived in Buenos Aires in search of economic opportunity. When these individuals joined the workforce, they created a working class that catapulted Argentina into position as one of the world's ten wealthiest nations as well as the cultural capital of Latin America. As the immigrant population began to grow, so did Buenos Aires's theater industry. Between the years 1900 and 1930, dozens of new theater companies emerged and began to replace the European touring groups thus far dominating Argentina's stages. Argentine theater historian, Beatriz Seibel, notes that, between the years 1900 and 1923, several new theatrical spaces were built across the nation, and theatrical attendance quintupled from 1.5 million attendees to 7.3 million. Part of the reason for the massive upsurge was that the theater became a space of acculturation and cultural integration, particularly in the development of the two most popular theatrical forms in early twentieth-century Argentina—the *sainete criollo*, and the *grotesco criollo*, representing the experiences of Argentina's marginalized and working-class immigrant population. Claudia Kaiser-Lenoir argues that the two forms represent complimentary components of the nation's immigration project: the *sainete* documents the building of community and integration of newly arrived populations, while the *grotesco* portrays the disillusionment of the migrant transition in Argentina.[2]

The *sainete* found humor in misunderstandings and conflicts between neighbors as a result of clashing immigrant customs. Sirena Pellarollo, in writing about the form, notes that the genre relied on comedic stock figures who lived in *conventillos*, the multi-family homes built in the settler neighborhoods of La Boca and Caminito.[3] Eventually, the neighbors

---

2 Claudia Kaiser-Lenoir, *El grotesco criollo: estilo teatral de una epoca* (Havana: Casa de las Americas, 1977).

3 Sirena Pellarollo, *Sainetes, cabaret, minas y tango. Una antología* (Buenos Aires: Corredor, 2001).

would overcome their cultural differences and return to a state of equilibrium and harmony as is the case in Florencio Sánchez's *Canillita* (1902) and Alberto Vaccarezza's *El conventillo de la Paloma* (1929). In contrast, the *grotesco* were dramatic works that depicted the strenuous realities of the immigrant experience, telling stories of transatlantic crossings, nostalgic longing, and economic anxiety (such as Armando Discépolo's *Mateo* [1923] and *Stéfano* [1928]). Ultimately, theater created a form of cultural consumption that empowered the immigrants to see themselves represented on stage as part of the national body.

By the 1930s, the immigrant narratives were replaced by Argentina's independent-theater movement, which increasingly turned toward international performance and production aesthetics. José Marial's history of the formation of Buenos Aires's independent theater notes that, as early as 1930, Leónidas Barletta, founder of Teatro del Pueblo, sought the cultivation of a new theatergoing public.[4] Major emerging playwrights, including Roberto Arlt, César Tiempo, Juan Oscar Ponferrada, and Carlos Gorostiza, began to address social concerns and vices through realistic plays that attempted to interpret the quotidian experiences of Buenos Aires' residents. Arlt's *Trescientos miliones* (1932), for example, depicts a domestic worker who daydreams about a large inheritance that will enable her to escape her dreary life. Carlos Gorostiza's production of *El Puente* (1949) shifted from the sentimental realism of the early independent theater toward a greater sociopolitical awareness, reflecting the nation's political fragility, economic decline, and increased demands for labor. Similarly, Osvaldo Dragún drew national and international attention with his play *Historias para ser contadas* (1956), influenced by expressionism and Brechtian-based *verfremdungseffekt*, made evident in its series of short scenes with political messages about abuse and economic corruption that called attention to Argentina's structural inequalities.

As political unrest, economic instability, and military violence intensified in the 1950s and 60s, theater artists continued to draw upon

---

4 Jose Marial, *El teatro independente* (Buenos Aires: Alpe, 1955)

international influences in their implementation of two distinct styles of theater—what acclaimed Argentine theater historian, Osvaldo Pellettieri, refers to as reflexive realism and the avant-garde.[5] Pellettieri defines the reflexive realists as a group of authors who concentrated their energies on the problems of the middle and working classes through social realism, drawing comparison to American writers such as Arthur Miller and Clifford Odets. Playwrights of this ilk, including Roberto Cossa, Ricardo Halac and Germán Rozemacher, through their dramaturgy, captured a sense of the middle-class Argentines' disillusionment and financial frustration. The avant-garde, on the other hand, distinguished themselves through theatrical pieces influenced by the Theater of the Absurd, the Living Theater's Happenings, and Artaud's Theater of Cruelty. Dramatists such as Griselda Gambaro, Ricardo Monti, and Eduardo Pavlovsky developed works characterized by a linguistic deconstruction and wordplay, themes of absence, and explorations of violence.

The military dictatorship of the 1970s and 80s and the accompanied threat of political violence created a precarious space for artmaking. Scholar Jean Graham-Jones notes that many theater-makers faced death threats and chose to go into exile before the dictatorship took hold.[6] Many Argentine playwrights, however, found opportunities to explore the nation's oppressive regime and its human rights abuses by crafting narratives that drew upon metaphor and myth. Roberto Cossa, Mauricio Kartun, and Susana Torres Molina were among those creating work during this moment of political hostility. As the political violence began to subside in the early 1980s, a group of authors and directors founded Teatro Abierto (1981–1985), a theatrical festival envisioned as an act of political resistance. During the festival's initial year, collaborators staged 20 one-act plays and drew over 250,000 spectators. The festival continued through the

---

5 Osvaldo Pellettieri, *Historia del teatro Argentino en Buenos Aires* (Buenos Aires: Galerna, 2005).

6 Jean Graham-Jones, *Exorcising History: Argentine Theatre under Dictatorship* (Lewisburg, PA: Bucknell University Press, 2000).

mid-80s until Raul Alfonsín's election restored democracy in Argentina and diminished demands for maintaining the project.

Following the restoration of democracy, many critics, scholars, and artists suggest that Argentine theater fell into a state of crisis. Theater artists failed to find a post-dictatorship discourse and aesthetic that could speak to contemporary political concerns without reverting to dualistic and simplistic conflicts between perpetrators and victims of violence. Theatrical attendance in Buenos Aires fell from 7 million spectators in the 1920s to just over 1 million in 1995. Although several important dramatists including Ricardo Bartís, Griselda Gambaro, Ricardo Monti, and Eduardo Pavlovsky continued their productive careers as playwrights and political critics even after the dictatorship was concluded, the nation's theater artists struggled to create performances that addressed Argentina's economic crisis, the nation's state of social unease, or the ongoing debate over transitional justice policies focused on reconciliation rather than retribution. Consequently, Buenos Aires's historically vibrant theaters began to lose their audiences while the nation's state-sponsored and commercial theaters became increasingly reliant on foreign productions, during what is widely considered a moment of national theatrical pessimism.

Ricardo Bartís describes Argentina's initial years of post-dictatorship theater as "broken," noting that the only recourse for theatrical reinvention was to create an alternative theater that could be produced in homes, basements, or other non-traditional spaces.[7] As Buenos Aires's theater became increasingly marginalized and impoverished in the 1990s, a group of artists developed their craft in precisely the sort of spaces that Bartís envisioned, creating projects that reflected their ongoing frustrations with the nation's sociopolitical and economic difficulties. These artists comprised the *teatro joven* generation, which includes Santiago Loza. Nevertheless, while *teatro joven* artists shared many similarities in terms of production aesthetics, artists and critics alike have rejected the notion that they belong

---

7 Bartís quoted in Jorge Dubatti, "El teatro en la dictadura: a 30 años de Golpe militar," *Picadero* 16 (2006): 19.

to a collective theater movement. The theater also began to take another shift as the realism and avant-garde debates of the mid-twentieth century began to give way. Pellettieri has written about an emergent postmodern "theater of disintegration," while Argentine theater scholar Jorge Dubatti suggests that the multiple approaches to theater-making emerging in the post-dictatorship era created a "micropoetics" of theatrical production that continues to exist in Buenos Aires to this day.[8]

But the 1993 election of Carlos Menem instilled a series of neoliberalist economic policies that coincided with the emergence of a budding generation of playwrights who began to revitalize the nation's theater and create new methods for theatrical activism. The country's failed neoliberal economic policies created socioeconomic crises, including a default on the country's foreign debt. Unemployment rose to 22.5% and millions of Argentines were underemployed. The peso was artificially devalued and over half of the nation was plunged into poverty. Twenty years after the start of Argentina's 1998 "Great Depression," its economy continues to face an inflation rate of over 25 percent annually, a devaluing of the peso and a collapse in foreign investment under the presidency of Alberto Fernández. Consequently, the nation's playwrights must continue to work with great resourcefulness and originality.

Contemporary Argentine theater's penchant for innovation and imagination is clearly reflected in Loza's work. Like many of his contemporaries, Loza works across theater, television and film, as writer, director, and producer. Loza's artistic education was predominantly based in Buenos Aires where he moved in 1995 to attend the National School of Experimentation and Cinematic Realization (ENERC) before enrolling in playwriting courses at the Metropolitan School of Dramatic Art. Unlike many of his peers, Loza hails from Córdoba and his spoken Spanish bears that accent,

---

8 Jorge Dubatti, *El nuevo teatro de Buenos Aires en la postdictadura (1983–2001)* (Buenos Aires: Centro Cultural de la Cooperación, 2002).

making him a bit of an outsider in the capital's artistic and intellectual circles. Loza's perceptions of occupying a marginal status are compounded by his self-described social anxiety, his queerness, and his surviving an oppressive religious education and nervous breakdown that silenced him for several years. All of these experiences have given him a personal insight into the outsider status that many of his characters share. Remarkably, from this point of view, Loza has produced many of the most successful plays performed in Buenos Aires in the last decade. His ability to blend emotional vulnerability and humor with storytelling creates geographic and cultural specificities through beautifully imagistic language.

Loza first came into the spotlight in the Buenos Aires Theater in 2001 when his short play, *Pequeña, Cruel, Bonita*, was selected as one of 41 plays for the Teatroxlaidentidad festival. This cycle of plays was sponsored by the Grandmothers of the Plaza de la Mayo in order to support their search for approximately five hundred children kidnapped by Argentina's dictatorship of the late 1970s and 80s. The play, a short monologue, received strong reviews for its evocative language and engagement with traumatic memories, and served as a precursor to the full-length dramatic works that won Loza larger acclaim and audiences. Loza's international reputation grew when his first feature film *Extraño* was selected for the Rotterdam International Film Festival in 2003 followed by his film *Los Labios* winning the "Un Certain Regard" prize at the 2010 Cannes Film Festival. He is also creator of the television series *Doce casas*, which received best series award at the 2014 Martín Fierro Awards. Despite Loza's growing reputation as a cineaste, he has continuously written for the theater, authoring approximately thirty plays over the course of his career. He has received national playwriting prizes from Argentina's Teatro XXI, Trinidad Guerrera, and Konex Letra, as well as nominations for the nation's ACE, Teatros de Mundo, Florencio Sanchez, and María Guerrero Awards.

In many ways, Loza builds upon Argentina's twentieth-century theater's traditions of representing the working-classes and marginalized people, whether through direct portrayals of their experiences or by documenting the voices of the bourgeois as they figure out how to live with the dispossessed. The plays featured in this anthology explore how working-class and marginalized individuals experience a reality very different from many of Buenos Aires's urban middle-class theater audiences in the hope that spectators might empathize with their experiences or at least consider the realities of a life that they do not know. Loza's dramaturgy focuses on seamstresses, orphans, ranch hands, and disaffected adults talking about their problems without any expectation of resolution. His plays augment the richness of Argentina's contemporary theater with dramatic situations and characters whose lives are complicated by the economic fallout caused by Argentina's adoption of neoliberal policies, the economic crash of 2001, the societal changes provoked by newcomers into a community, as well as the nation's rapidly changing viewpoints on race, gender identity, and sexuality.

The themes found in Loza's playwriting document the experiences of individuals who feel as though they no longer have a place in contemporary Argentine society. *Todo Verde* (2012), for instance, depicts a rural pastry chef and the turn her life takes for the worse with the arrival of another woman who brings outside knowledge that opens the community's hidden appetites. *Sencilla* (2009), co-written with Loza's longtime collaborator Lisandro Rodriguez, presents the story of two maids who find comfort in sharing their work experiences during the solitude of their half-hour smoke breaks. *Asco* (2010) allows an apartment doorman to articulate his isolation in spite of the countless residents who cross his path on a daily basis. In conveying the humor and pathos present in these working-class lives, Loza creates a connection between his dramaturgy and stories of the laboring class that have always been a part of the Argentine theater's connection to its audience, whether through the immigrant stories of the *sainete and criollo*, the reflexive realism of the 1950s and 60s, or the social concerns of the independent theater's formation that carry on through the post-dictatorship.

Rather than replicating and reinscribing the already-known narratives of Argentina's working people, however, Loza stages women whose stories have often been excluded on the national stage. His work is regularly sought after and performed by several of Argentina's leading actresses because of the sensitivity and attention to detail that he gives to women's stories. *Suspiros* (2012), co-written with Julio Chávez and Camila Mansilla, is a suspenseful thriller about seven women from the small city of Tandil who come to Buenos Aires to celebrate the marriage of one of their sons. But a series of mishaps born of frustration and resentment come to the surface, forever altering their lives. *Almas Ardientes* (2014) draws upon nine of Buenos Aires's most esteemed actress who explore their upper-middle-class privilege during the 2001 riots in Buenos Aires. The play shows Loza's other approach to documenting the underrepresented by noting the struggle of the basically good, but clueless bourgeois in the face of crisis. As the streets of Buenos Aires burn, the women must come to understand the interiority of their privilege and the frivolity of con-sumerism in times of economic precarity. *Todos las canciones de amor* (2016) reveals the emotional experiences of a mother and son reunited after a long separation, and the dreams, misunderstandings, and intensity born of absence and love, as the two resolve tensions surrounding the son's homosexuality and his relationship with a non-white boyfriend. Finally, *Un minuto feliz* (2016) captures the zeitgeist of Argentina's *Ni una menos* (not one more) campaign, a collective cry against gender violence, through its depiction of three generations of waitresses who must dress in miniskirts to work in a Buenos Aires cafe where they are repeatedly subject to sexual impropriety and misogyny.

The dramatic works selected for this collection represent several of Loza's best-known works in addition to smaller and more obscure plays that are deserving of a wider audience. The anthology also includes visual documentation of the playwright's many theatrical productions, and their historical and thematic contexts in the first English-language edition of his work. These plays were also selected for their legibility and producibility, particularly for directors outside of Latin America who are looking for an entry point into Loza's writing or into the contemporary Argentine theater. We invite readers to understand Loza's investment in the stories

of common laborers, his empathy toward women on the outskirts of society, and the poetic yet practical approach to playwriting that he employs
in order to ensure that his work is accessible and stageable for producers
not only in Argentina but also across the globe.

First in the anthology is Loza's most successful play *Nothing to Do
with Love (makes me envious)* [*Nada del amor me produce envidia*, 2008]
which explores the world of an introverted 1940s seamstress, one of Loza's
quintessential "silent women," whose ideas and stories blossom with life
when she is finally afforded the opportunity to share them. The Seamstress
works endless days in her studio where the play is set, buoyed by her
obsession with the musical performances of iconic Argentine film star
Libertad Lamarque. In a fantastical twist, both Lamarque and her real-life
long-time rival Eva ("Evita") Perón become aware of one of the Seamstress'
perfect dresses and compete for it. Loza envisions a playful alternative history where the fictitious beginnings of the long-time feud emerge via the
icons' interactions with the neighborhood Seamstress, who finds herself
at the heart of an epic conflict that threatens to destroy her. In the process,
she not only navigates between the two celebrities but also deeply recon-
siders her own relationship to her labor and to love in the context of the
complex dynamics of capital and power in the first Perón administration.
Performed as a monologue (often adding songs), *Nothing to Do with Love*
draws on Loza's uncanny knack for musicality in dialogue to capture the
frustrations of a pathologically quiet woman whose brush with celebrity
finally blows apart the doors of a circumscribed life, leading to a conclusion as thrilling as it is unexpected. *Nada del amor me produce envidia* has
been produced numerous times in Buenos Aires and in other cities
throughout Argentina in addition to receiving a staging in Toulouse,
France and a production by The Cherry Arts in Ithaca, New York in
March, 2017.

Winter Animals [*Pudor en animales de invierno*, 2011] has a fairly
conventional premise: An aging rural ranch hand travels to Buenos Aires
to spend a weekend with his troubled, bookish, and closeted son who
longs to forget his familial past. Loza complicates this family narrative

with surreal temporal shifts and a dream logic that upends expectations. The family reconciliation is made even more difficult by the presence of a naked woman who lives in the apartment's refrigerator and who roams the house as a witness to and salve for the son's emotional duress, as the father does his best to understand and accept this aspect of his son's lifestyle. Loza refuses to make a melodrama out of the tensions between father and son, whose histories of misunderstanding and miscommunication are palpable, if deep beneath the surface of conversations about seemingly mundane topics. Juxtaposed with what feels like scrupulous naturalism is an exploration of the complex fantasies and sexual obsessions of a young man looking to create a life of his own as his father searches emotionally for some reassurance that his son won't end up sad and isolated. Argentine reviewers compared this play to the work of Arthur Miller, but, in translation, echoes of Tennessee Williams emerge with equal power. The play uses time and the surreal to disrupt moments of realism in order to reveal what remains hidden through emotional obfuscation and sleight-of-hand. *Pudor en animales* ran for two years in Buenos Aires and was selected as part of the 8th Festival Internacional de Buenos Aires. The English translation premiered at the Cherry Arts in Ithaca, New York in March 2017. The translation was subsequently selected from over 100 submitted texts to close out "Global Queer Plays," a March 2018 festival of rehearsed readings produced by the Arcola Theater in London.

I Was Born to See You Smile [*He nacido para verte sonreír*, 2011] features a unique structural device. In real time, the audience witnesses the final interaction between a mother and son before the young man is taken to a mental institution. Miriam, the protagonist, searches for the right words to help her son understand what he has meant to her. In the process, she begins to unearth her own frustrations in raising a son who could not love her the way she wanted. As in many of Loza's plays, memories appear and disappear in words, gestures, and reactions. Miriam is at times exasperating, wildly misinterpreting her son's illness in a variety of ways, including cruel ones, as she attempts to understand the world in which she finds herself. Loza, however, works to help spectators sympathize with her in her efforts to explore the limits of her ability to say goodbye and to accept a mental condition that she cannot understand. In a particularly vivid simultaneous silent performance for the son, the audience watches the ambiguous reactions of a young man who perceives reality differently from others and who is unable to give his mother the sign she craves that he understands her needs. *He Nacido para verte sonreír* was presented by Madrid's Teatro de la Abadía in a successful production that was brought back in January 2018.

 Altitude Sickness [*El mal de la montaña,* 2013] focuses on four young adults, three men and a woman, discussing their concerns about life and love. Manu has just broken his engagement with Pamela, Ramo was recently left by his partner, and Tino cannot stop thinking about his dentist's secretary. Pamela is also present, and seems to have gone through a breakup, but as the four chat in an unidentifiable space across ambiguous moments in time, Loza's dramatic structure begins to feel disorientingly non-linear. Is Pamela the woman who figures in more than one of these stories? Or is she more than one woman? And/or are these three similarly named men actually just one man? Each of the characters is isolated in their own monologue. *Mountain Sickness*'s men and woman speak to each other with wit and charm but seemingly without regard for what the others are saying or how they are reacting, contributing to a dreamlike quality that pervades the play. This quality is amplified when, from time to time, a character shifts from a charming rumination on relationships to an anecdote about a shocking act of violence or cruelty toward the impoverished people always visible in the streets, as though an episode of *Friends* had suddenly gone strangely wrong. Ultimately, characters explore how they can manipulate their relationships in the service of their personal desires, even if only to guide them to a tranquil end. The play links the all-too-universal cruelties of love relationships to the unacknowledged daily cruelty of the radical economic inequality bred in late-capitalist societies. Co-translator Ariel Gurevich remarks that the play reveals the "casual fascism of the bourgeoisie." *El mal de la montaña* was produced in Buenos Aires under the direction of Cristian Drut.

This anthology concludes with another exploration of family bonds and a return to Loza's signature monologic form in *A Saint* [*La mujer puerca*, 2012], written for an unassuming woman of the working class. The titular character works at a convent, where she cares for the indigent elderly men who live their final days there, and her monologue is occasionally interrupted by the nonsensical but strangely potent gibberish of the resident to whom she speaks. The play considers the profound paradoxes of religious faith and the maintenance of piety in the face of overwhelming adversity. The orphaned protagonist is raised by an aunt who inscribes in her an overwhelming Catholic fervor that makes her pursue with single-minded determination the goal of becoming a saint. In spite of an intense and impeccable self-discipline, she finds that the task is easier to aspire to than to achieve, and her calling refuses to manifest itself. Initially, the narrative is a humorous portrayal of a character whose belief system justifies everything through religion and who barely apprehends the scientific or rational. As the story progresses, the protagonist's naivety gets her into more and more painful situations, as the limits of her socio-economic class collide with the strange purity of her religious convictions. The story finally turns toward the tragic as our protagonist grows more and more lost, until the sheer force of her desire seems to produce a mysterious apotheosis. Loza asks what it means to maintain a state of grace while devoting one's love and life to the unrequited service of an indifferent God in the face of impossible duress. *La Mujer Puerca* opened in Buenos Aires and has been brought back to the stage in every season since then. It has also been staged in Uruguay and in numerous cities across Argentina.

The plays in this anthology as well as the interview with the playwright that concludes this book show Santiago Loza as a versatile theater artist whose skill in portraying marginalized people with humor and pathos in the lived experiences of Argentines possesses a universality and confidence that carries the traditions of the Contemporary Argentine theater to audiences across the globe.

Noe Montez

The generation of Argentine theater artists working after the nation's 2001 economic collapse created performances in non-traditional spaces, including cultural centers, hotels, abandoned factories, nightclubs, and other venues that enabled them to present work inexpensively and without need for maximalist scenography. In 2008, Santiago Loza collaborated with playwright-filmmaker Lisandro Rodríguez as well as actors José Escobar and Mariano Villamarín. The group began working in an abandoned hardware store in the Palermo neighborhood of Buenos Aires, forming the Elephant Theater Club. The company remained in Palermo for four years before increasing rents forced the founders to look for a new home. In 2011, the company found a house in Buenos Aires's Almagro neighborhood, but did not have the financial capital to make the move. Loza and his collaborators needed to take on loans, sell family heirlooms, and draw upon their own personal savings in order to secure the site that became the Elephant Theater Club's new location. Although the theater was somewhat transient, the space became known as one of the most successful performance venues in Buenos Aires's independent theater circuit, and as a launching pad for Loza's career as a dramatist.

The story of Santiago Loza and the Elephant Theater Club is typical of Buenos Aires's independent-theater scene. Although these venues define the cutting edge of performance in the nation's capital, staging innovative and ambitious productions for audiences across the city, the theatrical pieces performed as part of the independent-theater often operate on a shoestring budget reliant on self-funding and clever promotion. Most productions are staged once or twice weekly, in theater spaces where eight to ten productions may be in performance during the week. Other theater artists look to build relationships with producers in Buenos Aires's commercial houses or with programming directors of major international festivals in hopes of staging their work for audiences across the globe.

In an interview with Santiago Loza conducted via email, the playwright reflected on his own career as a theater artist, as well as the ways that the city's independent theaters have survived economic and political changes.

NOE MONTEZ. When did you know that you were first attracted to the theater? What was the moment of revelation?

SANTIAGO LOZA. When I was a kid, drama attracted me. Telenovelas, tragedy, and the presence of good acting. The actors could make me believe anything. I liked watching television and going to the movies a lot more than playing or going to school. But there was never a revelatory moment, just a desire to escape the mundanity of childhood. Fiction and reading became my protectors. Even in adolescence, I knew that fiction could be an instrument to help me know the world. Fiction helped me understand the world and myself. Fiction transformed my life, and I'd like to believe that even as a young boy, I knew that it could give me a capacity to search for truth and to express myself in addition to entertaining.

MONTEZ. How did your upbringing in Córdoba influence your sense of aesthetics and the ways that you think about the theater?

LOZA. I am from the interior of the country, from the province. Being from the provinces and growing up there feels like growing up on the periphery. As a result, living in Buenos Aires feels somewhat foreign and one develops a feeling that one doesn't belong. The characters that I write about often share those same feelings, as if they're strangers in the environments that they inhabit. They all carry a certain discomfort.

When I was young and taking my first steps into the world of performance, I worked with a theater in Córdoba that was grounded in devised performance and a strong contempt for text. I didn't think that I would ever be able to dedicate myself to playwriting or to develop a writing profession. But when I came to Buenos Aires and began to study theater, I began to understand the value of the monologue and its internal logic.

MONTEZ. Buenos Aires is a hotbed of theatrical activity. How has your writing been informed by the experience of living and working in the capital? How has the independent-theater community particularly influenced your work?

LOZA. For those of us who came from the province, Buenos Aires was always a kind of Mecca. When I was younger and travelled to the city, I watched its theatrical output with amazement, especially the variety of productions staged within the independent theater. In those years—and even now—I was struck by the diversity of theatrical styles, the resourcefulness used in staging productions, the differences between Argentina's different production circuits, and the aesthetic experimentation offered by theater artists across the city. They enriched me, challenged my perceptions about what the theater could be. I'm not interested in being comfortable, so I take pleasure in the ways that the theater in Buenos Aires moves restlessly, in the ways in which it continues to challenge me.

MONTEZ. How does your writing reflect the economic and logistical realities of the Argentine theater industry?

LOZA. I don't know if I write theater that faithfully accounts for any reality. But I'm mindful of telling small stories, focusing on microworlds and containing narratives. These are plays that are financially easy to stage, both in Buenos Aires and in the provinces.

Otherwise my work is largely disconnected from any reality, although there are times when reality seeps in, in unexpected ways. Reality in Argentina is intense and ever-changing. It is impossible to abstract. I think my writing has an Argentinean air. At the same time, I try to avoid writing specifically about Buenos Aires or the provinces. I write stories that can be understood by even those who don't live or suffer in our reality.

MONTEZ. What is the difference between writing for the theater, writing for television, and writing for film?

LOZA. Film, television, and theater have different formats and audiences, so I build my work in each medium in different ways. In the theater, the plays I write are based on the written word and work with language. Whereas when I write for film and television, I am mindful that I have to write in a way that gives primacy to constructing images. Writing for television and film is grounded in movement in a way that writing for the theater is not.

MONTEZ. How do you begin a play? Do you start with an image, an emotion, or a theme that serves as the initial impetus for the work?

LOZA. A play comes intuitively to me. I never write from a theme, but certain phrases or images or emotions do appear to me in a blurred and enigmatic way. The initial impetus may not be very clear, but I try to specify the original impulse that informs my work and then act on it.

MONTEZ. Many of your works represent individuals who are on the margins of society. Why are you attracted to these characters? Would it be fair to say that this approach to character distinguishes you from other artists in Argentina?

LOZA. My characters live on the margins of society, but they are not completely outside of it. They are in the shadows and have personality characteristics that isolate them and remove them from the mainstream, but they are not criminals or human beings who have broken a social pact. It is their strangeness that isolates them and relegates them to isolation. I have deep empathy for such characters. I feel as though they are my equal, and vice versa. So, I try to write their experiences with deep tenderness and piety. I don't know whether this distinguishes me from other artists or not, but this is how I feel.

MONTEZ. You have often written works that are read as monologues. Why do monologues appeal to you as a vehicle for dramatic expression? How is the writing monologues different from writing dialogue?

LOZA. Writing monologues is just something that captivates me as a dramatist. I'm attracted to the idea of finding a particular voice and following it to its logical end. Dialogue creates a situation whereas one voice functions differently in performance. There's a flow of language and ideas in a monologue that carries its own logic. Sometimes that logic is very different from what I think and believe as an author, but I have to be faithful to that "other" that appears. I have to let go of my own voice in service of another.

MONTEZ. You are often credited for the sensitive way that you write women on the stage. Why are you so attracted to writing female protagonists and what gives you insight into the feminine psyche?

LOZA. I don't think in psychological terms. The characters appear as they are. Many times, women appear to me when I write. I don't ask them to appear, but they do. Maybe the feminine has a rawer and more vulnerable relationship with the primitive and crucial emotions of life, such as love and trauma. If that's true, then writing women allows me to reach places that writing men does not give me access to. But I'm not sure. My writing is intuitive, it happens instinctually. It also happens that I'm generally more attracted to the work of actresses on stage than I am the work of actors.

MONTEZ. Do you imagine your work as political? In what ways?

LOZA. If my plays are political, they are indirectly so, without referencing any specific agenda or policy. Maybe they are political through an acknowledgement of people on the margins, losers, and of those who have been humiliated.

MONTEZ. What role does humor play in your works?

LOZA. I believe in the transformative power of humor. It plays a pretty crucial role. It's a breath. A detour before returning to a darker area. It is a color that appears in some necessary way.

MONTEZ. What part does theater continue to play in contemporary Argentina? What is its social and cultural value?

LOZA. There's still power in the ability to express one's self in a hostile and adverse environment. I write alone, but the theater is meant to be a collective experience. There's always the possibility of an encounter with someone or something new. I'm someone who is naturally quite introverted. The theater allows me to communicate, to enter into a dialogue with others and get closer to them.

MONTEZ. What is universal about your plays that appeals to international audiences and that encourages programming directors to support your work?

LOZA. I don't know. I think at their core, my plays touch on topics that involve everyone: love, loneliness, death, laughter, what happens to us internally, and the secrets we dare not name. In spite of the fact that we live in different places, our internal experiences are similar and our feelings and emotions make us equals.

MONTEZ. Can you talk about the inspiration and the writing process of the works presented in this collection?

LOZA. *Nothing to Do with Love* [*Makes Me Envious*] arose from the desire to explore some of Argentina's mythical elements, namely, Eva Perón and melodrama, as recounted by a character who was fortunate enough to live in Buenos Aires during a moment when both were thriving. The work goes beyond the historical in order to capture an epic moment in the routine life of a working-class character. We learn about what happens to her when the unexpected and the extraordinary burst in upon her.

Winter Animals is about the relationship between a father and son. The audience feels the discomfort and fragility of their relationship while understanding why they can't address it fully. I also wanted to disrupt their relationship by adding a fantastic element in the woman who lives in the refrigerator.

I Was Born to See You Smile is the opposite of *Winter Animals*. It came from wondering what it must be like for a mother who must admit her son into a psychological facility. It's a work about the urgency of saying goodbye. But I also like this play because it touches on the subject of madness and what behavior exists beyond the limits of reason.

Altitude Sickness is perhaps the play that is most atypical of my work. The characters live in conflicts of love and existential crises. All of them are filled with loneliness as well as individual and social ruptures. It is a strange and enigmatic work, even by my own standards.

Finally, *The Saint* was inspired by images and anecdotes that came from my religious education, crossed with an interest in sharing the title character's extreme experiences of marginalization. The Girl wants holiness, but she can't escape the reality that her entire being is earthly. I remember the experience, feeling both enjoyment and suffering as I wrote the play.

Six Faces of the Seamstress

FIGURE 1.1 (LEFT) The original Seamstress: María Merlino, directed by Diego Lermán at Sportivo Teatral, Buenos Aires, 2008. Merlino sings in the style of Libertad Lamarque, and the play was commissioned to create a theatrical context in which she could perform Lamarque's songs. *Photograph by Maria Sureda.*

FIGURE 1.2 (BELOW) Luciana Mealla Cincuegrani, directed by Lucas Leiva at the Espacio Máscara, Cordoba, Argentina, 2015. *Photograph by Gastón Malgieri.*

FIGURE 1.3 (ABOVE) Soledad Silveyra, directed by Alejandro Tantanian at the Teatro Regina, Buenos Aires, 2012. *Photograph by Ernesto Donegana.*

FIGURE 1.4 (RIGHT) Virginia Méndez directed by Roberto Andrade at the Teatro del Anglo, Montevideo, Uruguay 2013. *Photograph by Natalia Delgado / Daniel Durán.*

FIGURE 1.5 (LEFT) Susannah Berryman directed by Norm Johnson, the Cherry Artists' Collective, Ithaca, NY, 2017. *Video capture by Al Grunwell.*

FIGURE 1.6 (BELOW) Gabriela Pérez Cubas, directed by Marcela Juárez at the Club de Teatro, Tandil, Argentina, 2015. *Photograph by Jesica Montagna.*

NOTHING TO DO WITH LOVE
[MAKES ME ENVIOUS]

A seamstress's room. In the middle of the space, a mannequin of a female torso with a wooden base. The SEAMSTRESS addresses it, talks to it. Looks at it. In the back a folding screen, a sewing machine.

SEAMSTRESS. Oh let's chitchat a little, or my tongue is going to simply dry out.

These things do happen. A tongue as dry as the desert!

One must move one's tongue, and exercise the throat, otherwise the sound would emerge so coarsely. Best to keep tuning things up. And you understand about fine-tuning. Hm, and you don't have a sex, do you? Well you are perfect for a chitchat.

I like the word "chitchat." The same way I like the word "locution," the way the "yoo" sounds: "locution." And I like the word "interlocutor" even better . . . as if the "yoo" were hiding in there: interlocutor . . . You are my interlocutor. Although for the most part I am one big ear, nodding my head while I do the hem. Well I always have pins squeezed between my lips! But pins or no pins, I just nod. Best to keep those lips closed, no words spoken here that should not be. Ever since I was a girl, that pin trick works a charm with the clients. And my goodness, you can hear just about everything around here—but I am a tomb. A tomb with pins! Pins like the flowers in the mouth of this tomb.

But now that the clients are gone, oh I'll take advantage and vibrate these cords. I don't know if you realize that when I talk, I'm vibrating cords.

Those cords nobody sees, but they do quiver . . . Like that time a man caressed my throat, and those cords shuddered out that wordless sound, that low dry moan, and I thought how mortifying. If he notices. How shameless. Traitorous cords.

Cords . . . like violin strings, guitar strings . . . the sort of strings that swell in the movies when couples touch. Not that strings like those sounded when I was touched. I suppose I was waiting for violins to envelop us, but the sound was of his breath close to my face—and that moan from my throat. I wasn't prepared, that must have been it, I was just a girl, I knew so little about all that business. Well, I haven't learned much more since then . . . It must have been the discomfiture of that moment that caused it never to repeat itself. It was during the carnival . . . after a dance . . . in a corner of the hall . . . My hair was covered with streamers and confetti and he offered to brush me off and I told him yes, of course, without knowing that his intentions for me weren't wholesome, well, that's how men are . . . He was very good looking . . . There against the wall, with his breath close, I could see him clearly . . . It must have been that moan from my throat that made him release me. As if he were afraid he'd choked me, he looked at me as he moved away and said something I didn't hear through the noise of the firecrackers some boys were setting off . . . I watched him as he ran away . . . And my throat remained almost feverish . . . For days I tied a silk handkerchief around it to ease that ache . . .

Well, I've gotten off the subject.

Cords. They say that everything happened because of those cords . . . I'm talking about her of course, about Libertad Lamarque. Her cords were so wonderfully fine, oh she sang like the birds, the voice of a dove, her voice just flew out like a little bird.

And this is how she made her throat so clear: I happen to know that Libertad gargles every morning with egg whites. That will do you good . . . and if it'll do you good, Libertad will do it! She must have somebody to crack a half a dozen eggs for her, separate the yolks from the whites, beat them, and warm them up for her to gargle.

That's why she has that voice of a bird, because of the clear part of eggs, it all comes together, if you know what I mean.

Goodness how funny . . . birds have wings just like angels do!

Or angels have wings like birds do, I don't know who got their wings first.

FIGURE 1.7 Soledad Silveyra, directed by Alejandro Tantanian at the Teatro Regina, Buenos Aires, 2012. This commercial revival of the play, a rare phenomenon in Argentina, dispensed with the dressmakers' dummy and realized her "espacio reducido" (reduced space). *Photograph by Ernesto Donegana.*

What I mean is, whenever I think of Libertad, I think of her as an angel.
It must be because of angels that I like tulle and wedding dresses . . . All
white and ethereal . . . The immaculate bride held up by cherubims with
little velvety bottoms.

The immaculate bride. Well.

I've made dresses for brides who had been tainted, one does notice
these things . . . When I fit the dress, I sometimes find a biggish belly, and
if one is canny one doesn't need to be told . . . I always figured out a way
to hide those girls' predicament . . . Show them to advantage, avoid gossip
. . . There's always a pleat, a frill, some needlework to conceal that kind of
thing. I'm an expert at that, don't you know . . . at keeping all kinds of
secrets. Let's just say you get accustomed to it . . . In the end, clothes are
for concealing the flesh.

Well one can't simply go around in one's birthday suit, how horrible,
that's what clothes are for! I was always a bit frightened of naked bodies,
that's why I have that screen, so they can change on the other side. But
some of them march right in . . . As if I didn't exist and they were alone in
front of a mirror . . . That happens too . . . Ceasing to exist, that happens.

Like dead people. Well, that's what they say. It happens when they
wake up from death, that's the story. At the very moment their mortal eyes
close, in the same room open the eyes of the soul. They find themselves
there, in the room they just left, but without people. They walk around
the house . . . unpeopled. They go out onto the street . . . unpeopled. The
life of things but not of people. Not of them as people either, but they don't
realize that yet. Now they are . . . unpeople. Ghosts.

It's hard to get used to being a ghost.

Goodness how funny. I'm getting chills!

They want to drink water but they can't hold onto the glass, they try
to open the door but they can't grasp the knob. The new life of the dead is
terribly difficult. It's only when they realize they've stopped existing on
this side that they find peace. In the meantime, they go on testing their
absence, the limits of a ghost.

FIGURES 1.8–9 A different relationship to the dressmakers' dummy: Gabriela Pérez Cubas, directed by Marcela Juárez at the Club de Teatro, Tandil, Argentina, 2015. *Photographs by Marina De Pian.*

That's what the noises are, the cries.

That's why I get frightened.

I am.

I exist.

I've gotten off the subject.

Brides cease to exist . . . That's what the dress is for. She ceases to be the maid she had been . . . and later, she ceases to be the bride and becomes . . . well. The dress is used only that once. It's made for the single women to envy. And for the husband to enjoy opening up, parting the fabrics. That's why a good wedding dress should have a lot of layers, so it takes some effort for the husband to get to the final layer . . . I mean to the . . . center.

Sometimes they bring the dress back simply torn apart, and I ask what happened, and they say the husband was impatient, and that seems so peculiar to me . . . I've seen fellows with the faces of angels who have torn that dress shamefully.

It is shameful that they don't take care of something that cost some-body so many sleepless nights. That in their lust they couldn't value a body's hard work.

And I don't say that because I'm envious.

Nothing to do with love makes me envious.

That's why I like angels . . . Because they're clean and white and don't know a thing about lust.

Like Libertad. "The bride of the Americas." A bride in white who remains virginal for all eternity . . . A bride free of sex singing barefoot across the continent, smiling down from a silver screen, with that voice that would break borders . . . Libertad, loved by all men . . . Libertad, filled with light . . . You're the one to whom I pray. The immaculate bride of the cinema matinée . . . I sing your songs till I'm sick with them. No, I don't have envy . . . Envy is something else . . . Something that can't be hidden

. . . Like the stain that . . . well, the white dress, you know, some brides, the next morning.

Envy . . .

Love . . . Always talking about love. I don't know what they see in it. What in the world do they see in love . . . clients always talking about those things . . . Songs of love all sound the same. Those tangos . . . All that doomed, hopeless love . . . "Love . . . "

Love itself, and the word "love."

Love is that thing that's always happening to other people.

And the word, well, it seems sticky to me . . . As if it stayed stuck to the roof of your mouth when you said it. Love . . . Things actors in dark glasses do. For single women, like me, love is something more modest . . . I mean, the things I can do with these fabrics, my ability to stitch and unstitch, to imitate a dress from a Parisian shop window without having ever set foot in Europe, to remember when Libertad came here and I took her measurements with my own trembling hands . . . That's love . . . A love without a man . . . It's the love of the seamstress . . . You understand me . . . Because you're neutral, you're here and you're not here, and that doesn't scare me.

You're my interlocutor. With that "yoo" still hiding inside.

And I'm the single lady who makes dresses for all the girls in love.

What a tragic role I was written in this farce.

But back to facts, don't you know done is done.

There's a time to stop weaving and cut to the subject, and I am an expert of the cut, in fact I'm a cut above.

Goodness how funny, cutting to the subject of cutting that fabric.

I had never seen fabric like that. The day they brought it I thought (and I was not wrong), that fabric marked a before and after in my life . . . I mean my professional life, the life I lived between these walls. As though something was going to happen in here, as if some important part of the world was installing itself right in the middle of this room . . . I realized

FIGURE 1.10 (LEFT) María
Merlino, in the world prèmiere
production directed by Diego
Lermán at Sportivo Teatral,
Buenos Aires, 2008.
Photograph by Maria Sureda.

FIGURE 1.11 (BELOW) Susannah
Berryman, in the first production of this translation.
Directed by Norm Johnson at
the Cherry Arts, Ithaca, NY,
2017. *Video capture by Al
Grunwell.*

that before I'd even touched the fabric and asked who the dress was going to be for.

I'd like to stop for a moment here, with the fabric. I'm going to stop because in that moment everything stopped.

You know, I went to the theater once, and saw this: for a few moments, everything on the stage went dark and one single light, very focused, illuminated a person, and one understood: everything had stopped, this person exists and does not exist. Present and absent at the same time.

That happened to me with the fabric.

Or something like that . . . When I caressed the fabric, it was as if my sense of touch had been asleep for years and was waking up clean and young . . . It was a pleasure that began in the palm of my hand and spread through the rest of my body.

Threads of a silk I had never known, the product, definitely, of an Orient that only exists in outlandish stories . . . When I touched it, I felt the tiny hands of the girls who collected the cocoons of the silkworms . . . the worn hands of the old women who spun the thread on wooden wheels at the side of a river of transparent water . . . the rough hands of the men who folded and rolled the fabric on a bamboo pole . . . the beaten hands of those who transported it in a boat . . . the tobacco-smelling hands of the man who will finally caress the dress . . . the coarse hands of the maid who will wash it with care and with envy . . . the dirty hands of the beggar woman who after many years, when it's become rags, will push it in with the other rags until it disintegrates into filth . . . and the infinitesimal hands of the grubs as they devour it to make another cocoon . . . and so on . . .

Something about all those hands in my hand, something about the infinite, made me caress the fabric and ask again, because I hadn't been listening, who will the dress be for? If he'd told me I couldn't hear it, or couldn't believe it. Libertad, it's for Libertad, he said.

Libertad, who slapped Evita? That Libertad? The one who sings with the voice of a canary?

Libertad, in the flesh.

In moments like that one feels sort of diminished, you understand what I mean, let's say one feels small. The way I repeated "Libertad" had something to do with that, as though I were saying who am I that she should come here and I should take her measurements? And adjust the sleeve, and see the defects of her body and regard those defects and forget those defects, which is what one is paid to do.

That's what I mean when I say one can feel small.

I'm not saying one always feels like that, let's say one can forget oneself, I mean, there isn't always time to think about smallness or bigness because there's always a delivery to be made, a wedding, a saint's day, a quinceañera, you understand. You, standing right there you know that sometimes one loses oneself, and there's no day or night. There's just delivering the dress in shape and on time. And to that, you are the only witness—you, and the rings around my eyes.

And then someone arrives, and proposes a dress for Libertad. And the word Libertad is so big that one feels small.

And when they left me alone . . . I sat down and my heart simply fell. I looked at the fabric from a distance and I felt sad. I'm not going to be able to make this dress because these things are important . . . to make a dress like that is like fulfilling a mission from destiny, if there is such a thing as destiny . . . I'm saying that these things don't just happen, that folks come into this room and . . . I fell silent for hours. Still. As though I were defeated.

How could she give her a slap like that if she was so tiny.

You only had to see her to realize she'd be incapable of hitting anybody.

And what's more, if she were going to go against Eva, that would be like going against the General, and nobody goes against the General . . . And I don't say a thing about the General, not alone to these walls nor to the clients, when they bring up the General I pretend I don't hear, I concentrate on other things . . . It's not that I'm against him, nor in favor. I'm not in favor nor against, it's all the same to me, it's all the same to me what he does with the workers and the factories, what does all that change for

FIGURE 1.12 (TOP) Silveyra in the Tantanian production, Buenos Aires, 2012. *Photograph by Ernesto Donegana.*

FIGURE 1.13 (BOTTOM) Berryman directed by Johnson at the Cherry Arts, 2017. *Video capture by Al Grunwell.*

me, it doesn't change anything, my life is the same with the General or without the General . . . But that's something one doesn't say . . .

I'm getting ahead of myself. Being forced to decide, I thought it would never happen to me. But let's go step by step. First you cut the pattern, don't you know.

The day Libertad came my legs were shaking, I'd spent the whole night cleaning, feather-dusting all over the place, it seemed to me this room should be clean, clean, clean, as impeccable as she looks, in the movies.

I put on my very best ensemble to receive her.

Oh, I forgot the most important thing: the dress was ready. Or almost ready, a couple of tweaks, and ready. And, modesty aside, I had done honor to the fabric. It was a little morsel of perfection.

I put it in the middle of the room, there where you are. I moved my reading lamp close and aimed the light so you could really see it. So you'd notice.

It was a dress for a queen. As though if Argentina had a queen, at some point she absolutely would have worn that dress. But this isn't a country of queens, too much wind and dust for a queen, too much wildness, not enough fine folk, don't you know.

It's not that my clientele is precisely common, but fine folk, really fine? Few and none.

Libertad came the closest to what a seamstress like myself might think of as elegant.

She was little, but she had elegance.

I mention how little she was because the moment I saw her, I felt a bit disillusioned.

Movies make things bigger. I don't know, as though people in movies weren't of human stature, as though they were giants. I don't know, there's something . . . disillusioning at first. While I was measuring her, I thought, well in the end what's all the fuss, she's flesh and bone don't you know, nothing spectacular, no sir.

But afterwards it turned the other way around. She had something about her gaze, or her way of moving. I asked myself what it was she had . . . What did she have? . . . Well she had elegance, that's what.

I thought, in Europe, women must all be like her. Maybe a little taller, but one could imagine women just like that, elegant, smoking on the Champs-Elysées . . . That's what elegance is . . . Dresses fitted to the body and that delicate walk. As though stepping and not stepping at the same time. As though to step on the earth was something . . . something vulgar. Something mundane.

She was very Argentine and very European at the same time, I don't know if you follow, because I do want to get to the heart of the thing.

Tiny and elegant. She barely directed a word to me. I asked her if it pleased her, if the dress was to her liking. She didn't say yes or no, she said something needs to be changed. Something. She said "something . . . " Like that, unspecifically . . .

To me, the dress was perfect, it didn't have a single flaw, it was the best these hands had ever made. So I lifted my head, because I was kneeling down, and from down there the word just slipped out "why?" . . . I heard myself asking it, almost insolently . . . Well the silence was like a tomb. I regretted it, I swear I regretted the question but it was too late, the word had escaped my mouth and she half-closed her eyes and in the middle of that silence she murmured: I'm not sure . . . It could be a dress for that Eva Perón.[1]

That's what I think I heard.

Oh I should have bit my tongue 'til it bled, to never speak again, chop my words clean off.

I saw her let her face fall, like this, to one side . . . just like in the movie *Bewitching Kisses*, before she sings what she sings . . . as if a part of her were fainting. Not a complete faint, a semi-faint, a halfway-to-a-faint. And from the depths of that body came that voice.

---

1 In the original, "la Duarte."

FIGURE 1.14 (LEFT) Cubas in the Juárez production in Tandil, 2015. *Photograph by Marina De Pian.*

FIGURE 1.15 (RIGHT) Silveyra in the Tantanian production, Buenos Aires, 2012. *Photograph by Ernesto Donegana.*

One believes nothing extraordinary can happen in this life. I mean to say, I know what kinds of things I can expect. It's like with the clients and the patterns: they talk to me, and I can already see the dress, and the dress I see in my mind isn't so different from the final dress. I'm not sure if I'm explaining myself.

As if nothing could truly be a surprise . . . I mean that everything, and by that I mean everything, must fall within what is possible.

This is what I mean: I am a neighborhood seamstress. One doesn't have to be clairvoyant to know the future of a seamstress.

So the day Libertad came, I felt . . . Well I felt, like an electric jolt in my body, that something extraordinary had happened . . . I mean, look at what can happen! And when she left and I was here alone . . . I felt with an even greater violence in my body that the moment was over . . .

I mean to say, the extraordinary cannot be planned, but it also cannot be repeated.

Now, all this I'm saying about the extraordinary is what I thought about the encounter with Libertad. And I kept thinking that, for several days . . . Without realizing, without knowing how wrong I was.

Because the extraordinary, when it happens, installs itself with a force that throws open an unknown door, a new one, through which it can return . . . I don't know if I'm explaining myself . . .

I'll take myself as an example, since just around here there are no other examples.

I was here. The dress was ready. Libertad had decided it was perfect, after all.

There was a knock at the door and a man advised me that la Señora had heard of my fame . . . What fame? I said, thinking they were pulling my leg . . . Your fame, he said very seriously. La Señora is in the car . . . Can we keep this in confidence? What Señora?, I said . . . La Señora, he said, is there more than one? . . . And in that moment I saw her descend from the car. Now, I never use that word "descend," in any other case I'd

say: "she got out of the car" and that's that. But she didn't get out . . . she
descended, in the same way angels descend in dreams and kiss us on the
forehead.

She was an apparition that had nothing to do with this world.

The moment I saw Evita come into my workshop I believed that I had
died, that it was all part of what they say happens in the Life Eternal.

It was an . . . I must have eternity on my mind. It was an eternity
before I could speak again, babble a single word that made sense.

She walked all around the room . . . I thought: how can someone
do so much walking in such a small space? . . . She touched the fabrics,
studied the seams.

What may I do for you, Señora?, I dared to ask.

Silence.

In the center of the room was the dress for Libertad, glowing, just
finished.

She stopped. Looked at it for a long time.

How much?, she asked me.

It's for a client, I told her.

That's not what I asked you. I don't want to repeat the question.

It's not for sale . . . It's for a client. I can make you one just like it.

I don't want one just like it, I want that one.

My legs were shaking. I needed air.

It's not finished, it needs . . .

What does it need? she interrupted.

Time (I would have liked to say), I need time, to understand this, but
I didn't say anything, I remained quiet.

The man with her was wearing a dark grey suit, and an embroidered
handkerchief protruded from his pocket, I hadn't remarked it before, that's
what I was noticing when he put himself between la Señora and me and
extended his hand with an envelope that said "confidential information."

SANTIAGO LOZA

FIGURES 1.16–17 Berryman directed by Johnson at the Cherry Arts, 2017. The dress in this production was abstracted as a wall of red and orange tulle. *Video captures by Al Grunwell.*

I opened it, I was trembling, and on a page of letterhead bearing the presidential seal, somebody, some bored secretary, had typewritten some encoded numbers. I immediately realized: they were Evita's measurements. As I glanced at the page, the one thing that caught my attention was that she had such a small bust . . . Evita was actually quite flat-chested.

These trivialities . . . These things one fixates on and afterwards forgets. Well I'm talking about details, I do get fixated on details. And a preoccupation with detail makes all the difference in this job.

It's not that I'm better than so many others, what makes me different is that I am a detail person.

You know, I believe life is made of details, and we are what connects them . . . the way two scraps of fabric are married to create something whole.

I am the details.

The heat that remained in my hand after Eva squeezed it to say goodbye . . . She shook hands firmly, like a man, with that kind of force.

With my clients, we kiss when they leave me, let's say there's a certain family feeling. A kiss on the cheek and see you later.

But she offered me her hand, and I'd stretched out my face as a reflex, as though to give a kiss on the cheek, but she extended her hand, and there I am hanging, my neck stretched out and my body leaning toward her, well I almost lose my balance without the support of the other cheek, don't you know. I almost fall on my face . . . goodness how funny, for a moment I pictured myself discarded on the floor at Eva's feet, crawling like a creature from the swamp. Yes . . . I felt as though I were another species, not human, when she gave me her hand, a . . . a pest, yes, that's what we call those creatures. She didn't look me in the eye, only squeezed, and I could feel the bones of her hand . . . The consciousness of the bones of the hand. Do you know one doesn't notice bones until they cause pain? As though bones existed and didn't exist, until they tighten, hard . . . This consciousness of animals and of bones, all this happened to me.

That's the good thing about this room not having windows.

It doesn't cross one's mind until something like this happens. After Eva left, I thought, what a blessing I don't have a window.

Because if anyone had seen me in that moment they would have been terrified. For enclosed in this place was not a humble seamstress . . . No, it was that creature I mentioned before. A thing that wasn't human.

A she-beast of an unknown species.

My mouth was foaming . . . My eyes were white, I dragged myself into the corners . . . Clawed the fabrics . . . Chewed the wood of the chair . . . You can see, all those marks over there.

I had become animal.

That must be what madness is, to abandon all one's manners.

When everything was overturned, thrown into an impossible disorder, when there was no further way to discompose this room I fell still, panting, sweating.

And in front of me, there, the dress. Resplendent.

I can't choose, I thought, if I give it to Libertad, it will be my perdition . . . If I give it to Eva, I will be damned for centuries and centuries.

When I talk about the extraordinary, I'm also talking about the fatality that comes afterwards . . . About the misfortunes that follow. . . About the price that must be paid when the marvelous enters a space as reduced as this one.

And I am not one of the people who decide.

The world is made of two classes of people: those who decide, and those who comply.

I belong to the second category.

Oh, you may say I decide on cuts, some shapes, but I reply I do not. Perhaps I share in the decision of a client, but decide, no, I've never decided.

Not even as a girl did I ever decide, I always said, "alright." Nodding my head like so, lowering my gaze, avoiding the eyes, all the things

FIGURES 1.18–19 Cubas in the Juárez production in Tandil, 2015. *Photographs by Marina De Pian.*

obedient people do. Resentfully on occasion, oh my yes, but our very gestures conceal that.

And having to decide between two loves, between the love of one man or another . . . like in those stories . . . well, that never happened to me.

We're different kinds: Libertad and Eva one kind, and I another . . . Though things sometimes get confused.

I'll explain . . . Power, is the thing . . . To decide has power . . . The power to be able to do. That day, in that room . . . When I was left alone, I felt the really extraordinary thing wasn't Eva's visit, nor the encounter with Libertad. It was something else . . . It was that for the first time, here, alone in front of that dress, the one who had the power was I.

And that's what happened: I said "I" in the silence . . . at other times when I'd said "I" it was like nothing, as if the word had no weight, as if it floated and there was no need to say "I" because "I" didn't signify anything.

But this time, when I said "I" I felt it, with force, with weight and power.

I made that dress.

I can deliver it to Eva, or to Libertad.

I will triumph as a designer for presidential galas.

I will be the woman everyone talks about, the fought-over dressmaker who creates the dresses everybody desires.

I . . . I . . . I repeated "I" something like eighty times . . . and as I repeated it, the force that it had was being lost. Was draining away.

I, I finally said, alone with my soul, what will I do with my decision?

At the end of the day, we all wait a lifetime to decide things like this, and when they happen we aren't ready . . . As if the body were at war with itself, and in pain . . . And the only desire one can feel is for everything to

FIGURE 1.20 (FACING PAGE) Silveyra in the Tantanian production, Buenos Aires, 2012. *Photograph by Ernesto Donegana.*

be done. For whatever happens to happen and for everything to return to the way it was before. The same. With my insubstantial "I" and everything.

So I closed the doors.

All the doors.

I dragged furniture against the doors to block them, so nobody could force them, or at least it would be harder to do so.

I looked at the disarray left in the wake of my rapture.

In the center, there where you are, the dress remained still. A mute witness to my madness.

And what I did then is my secret—I'm telling it to you, who won't judge me . . . Who won't say even a peep . . . A tomb, you heard me, a tomb—

As if madness had possessed me, my clothing, this modest outfit was burning on my body.

Nobody's here, I told myself, nobody's here, I'm alone, and no sooner had I told myself that than I undressed.

It's not that I'd never been naked, I do that every second day to take a bath, but only there, with the tap running, and quickly so as not to waste water.

But I'd never been naked without a reason.

There I was, and naked like a crazy person I danced all around that room.

I sang the way Libertad sang, I sang for myself, as nobody had sung for me nor will ever sing for me.

I saw my naked body in that mirror.

And then I approached the dress, and slowly, like somebody savoring an evil deed, I began to put it on . . . Slowly, very slowly . . . Allowing the fabric to caress me.

I straightened up, upright, lifting my head toward the ceiling. And from an angle, I saw myself in the mirror and . . . what astonishment.

FIGURE 1.21 Méndez in the Andrade production, Montevideo, 2013. *Photograph by Natalia Delgado / Daniel Durán.*

I wasn't seeing a neighborhood dressmaker in disguise, no, what I saw was a queen, driven mad.

That old saying—you can dress a monkey in silk but a monkey it will remain—is a lie, let me dress that monkey and I will transform it into a princess. Nobody will ever suspect there's a little monkey at the center of all that beauty.

And it wasn't just that I felt like a queen, I also felt the loneliness of rulers. The silence that remains when the subordinates have left, the trembling after all the orders have been delivered, the disgust that grows from that accumulation of flatteries . . . That solitude of queens . . . I could see it in them. In the depths of each of them. I didn't notice it when they were here, only after, when I remembered them. Libertad and Eva were alone, I thought. All those men, all those jewels, all that tribute for nothing, I thought . . . So many things, to wind up quarreling over this dress.

Maybe it's simply a way to comfort oneself, but at times one must think about that sort of thing. The loneliness of other people.

I thought all that wearing the dress, dripping with sweat.

And then I said to myself, I'm not going to give it to them. Not to one nor the other. This dress is mine—like this moment—so secret and so mine that I'm not going to give it to anybody.

And I had those flasks of alcohol, to get out spots. And those perfumes, and don't tell anybody because everyone thinks it was an accident, but while I was dancing, wearing the dress, I began throwing them all over the place . . . Emptying the jars and continuing the dance and the deep smell of the alcohol was dizzying and I swear that if happiness exists it must be something like that and it was only a question of taking a simple match, I tossed it there where you are, and the happiness became a bonfire . . . You're going to tell me I was crazy and I can't deny that, but that's how I danced, with that dress of fire, among the fabrics that were being consumed the way passionate loves are consumed.

I danced until the fire had devoured me. They're so alike, heaven and the inferno . . . I swear I can still see that fire, and there must be something that purifies us in every flame . . . Because afterwards . . . When the fire had gone out . . . And only cinders and embers remained . . . They didn't find a thing, not the remains of dresses nor pieces of my body . . . Everything had been consumed . . . Up in smoke.

Some doubted I had ever existed. Others said I'd run through the streets like a human torch, that I fell in the river where the water extinguished me and the current dragged me out to sea . . . Others said the fire concealed the evidence of dark dealings that had happened by night in this room, they talked of clandestine gambling and exotic drugs . . . Others said the fire was a way to escape my double life as a dressmaker by day and prostitute by night . . . But all those stories died out just the same as the fire.

They all became the same, in forgetting.

Libertad and Eva, too, quickly forgot me.

And one day they forgot one another.

Eva—well, everybody knows what happened.

Libertad lived a long life, and went far away.

And I . . .

It's hard to imagine one could be this happy.

To imagine that perfect joy happens in one moment of rapture, and afterwards the void . . . And you are with me in that void. In this small paradise . . . This eternal life stitching and unstitching . . . The reduced heaven of the seamstresses.

Eternity.

I'm not alone . . . You are with me.

THE END

Nothing to Do with Love

TRANSLATOR/EDITOR'S NOTE

Most of Loza's monologuing women address a more-or-less silent onstage interlocutor rather than the audience. The text of *Nada del amor me produce envidia* indicates that the Seamstress is addressing her dressmaker's dummy, using the informal pronoun "vos." The first production I saw was directed for the Buenos Aires commercial stage by Alejandro Tantanian, now the Artistic Director of Teatro Cervantes. With Loza's blessing, Tantanian eliminated the dummy and addressed the play to the audience. To effect this change in Spanish required cutting the explicit references to the dummy and replacing the Argentine second-person singular "vos" with the plural "ustedes." In English, "you" can be either singular or plural, so the translation happily needn't decide whether the speaker is addressing the dummy, the audience, or some magical combination of the two.

In drafting this text, I was fortunate to spend two work sessions with Tantanian, sessions that revealed something to me about the sympathies between the jobs of theater director and theater translator. When discussing individual moments, rather than talking about imagery or language, Tantanian spoke quite naturally about action. The Seamstress says that *in order to*. Each speaking became a motivated doing.

Plenty of ink has been spilled on how different theater translation is from other forms of literary translation: a translated play wants to be maximally understandable on one hearing; ideally it wants to feel legible enough in the destination culture to justify the time and budget of production; and so on. For me, those sessions with Tantanian added to that list how useful it is to think of even the most seemingly poetic work for the stage not simply as a series of ideas, but as a series of *actions*.

Tantanian is also a renowned translator of English-language work into Argentine Spanish. (While we met, he was taking time out from working on a translation of *Anything Goes*.) Tantanian thinks of the Seamstress, whose voice is distinctively old-fashioned, as being something like an Argentine version of a Tennessee Williams heroine. So without evoking any specific US regional accent, Ariel and I aimed for a Williams-esque rhythm and resonance.

The play's heroine is torn between two icons who might have been thought of as allies to working-class women: the populist politician Eva Perón and the popular entertainer Libertad Lamarque. Many productions of this play have incorporated these figures into the *mise en scène*. Tantanian's began with a video prologue evoking the two; Diego Lerman's Spanish-language premiere incorporated Lamarque's songs, performed by the actress; and in the Cherry Artists' Collective English-language premiere, images of the women were incorporated into the set.

Evita needs no introduction. Lamarque was a film actress and tango singer whose career spanned from the 1930s through the 1970s. It is a measure of how famous Libertad is in Argentina that early in the play, where the translation reads, "I'm talking about her of course, about Libertad Lamarque. Her cords were so wonderfully fine" the Spanish text merely says, "I'm talking about her of course, whose cords were so wonderfully fine" and the audience knows that the Seamstress can only be speaking of Lamarque.

WINTER ANIMALS

A tiny apartment. A kitchenette, one door to the bathroom, one to the hall. A fridge. A TV on a trunk. Not much more, there's no room. FATHER and SON preparing the trundle bed for the night. They pull out the lower mattress and arrange it beside the other, they put on the sheets.

SON. Mom's good?

FATHER. Working, like always. You know how she is.

SON. Yeah, I know. Never stops.

FATHER. Never stops. You know . . .

SON. Yeah, I know, poor Mom—

FATHER. Like a machine.

SON. Batteries never run down.

FATHER. No, never do . . .

SON. She didn't say if she's gonna come?

FATHER. Last time she spent the whole time cleaning.

SON. I didn't ask her to.

FATHER. It's beyond her control. She can't stop.

SON. Better she doesn't come.

FATHER. Yeah, better.

SON. Didn't even go out for a walk.

FATHER. She must have gone to Mass.

SON. Yeah, Mass every evening, she did that.

FATHER. She's getting more and more religious.

FIGURE 2.1 (PREVIOUS PAGE) Dean Robinson and Johnny Shea in the first production of this translation of *Winter Animals*. Directed by Samuel Buggeln, produced by the Cherry Arts, Ithaca, NY, 2017. *Photograph by Samuel Buggeln.*

SON. She prays a lot, she starts to pray and doesn't stop.

FATHER. That much praying gives me a headache. I dunno. Opposite's happening to me.

SON. What's that?

FATHER. Time goes on, I believe less and less.

SON. You're not gonna be cold with just one blanket?

FATHER. Nah, I don't usually get cold. What do you call people who don't get cold?

SON. I don't know what they're called, I think fakirs.

FATHER. That's the Indians that don't feel pain. I'm talking about cold.

SON. Sort of the same feeling, cold and pain.

FATHER. Look at you, deep thinking. I was talking about the illness, where you can't feel cold. Like that story I used to tell you when you were little, the five knights who had special powers—one tall, one superstrength, one that didn't feel cold . . .

. . . That was very funny, the five knights that helped the prince with his five tests. One tall, the super-strong one, the one that didn't feel cold . . . No, it was heat he couldn't feel, he could feel cold . . .

It was the opposite of that disease. Because he had to survive one night inside a bonfire. There he was, dying of cold, right in the middle of the flames . . .

. . . You must've thought that story was pretty dumb.

Even more so now, all the things you're reading.

SON. I don't even know which story that is.

FATHER. One I used to tell you, but I can't remember the powers of the knights I left out . . .

SON. I said I don't remember.

FATHER. If you don't remember you don't remember. Wasn't that important.

SON. You want to take a shower?

FATHER. Can't be that important if I can barely remember myself.

   . . .

Today when I got here. You were in the bathroom, I opened the fridge to get some water and there was a naked woman in there.

SON. I already saw her.

FATHER. What's she doing in the fridge?

SON. I dunno . . .

FATHER. Maybe she needs a coat.

She'd be better off getting into bed.

SON. No, the cold makes her feel better.

FATHER. I never would've thought.

SON. What?

FATHER. That I'd find my son with a woman in the refrigerator.

SON. I barely know her.

FATHER. She seems nice.

SON. If you're going to take a shower better to do it now, later the pipes make noise and bother the neighbors.

FATHER. To think I used to tell you all those stories from memory. And the ones I didn't remember I made up.

Now I don't even have an imagination.

SON. I'll turn on the shower for you. It'll heat up the bathroom a little so you won't get cold.

FATHER. I don't really feel like taking a shower, bother you if I don't?

SON. No, why would it bother me?

FATHER. Bothers your mother.

SON. She likes cleanliness.

FATHER. Sometimes I'm in the shower and I'm already clean and I ask myself, why am I washing?

SON. Sometimes it's a question. If you want to put on your pajamas, you can do it in the bathroom.

FIGURE 2.2 Ricardo Félix and Martin Shanly in the world premiere production of the Spanish original, directed by Lisandro Rodriguez, produced by the Elefante Club de Teatro, Buenos Aires, 2011. Part of the eighth Festival International de Teatro de Buenos Aires (FIBA), the production was on an elaborate two-story set. *Photograph by Nora Lezano.*

FATHER. Your mother forgot to pack my pajamas.

Bother you if I sleep in my underwear?

SON. How's it gonna bother me.

I don't wear pajamas either.

FATHER. Better that way. I'm going to the bathroom.

SON. Don't have to ask my permission.

SON is left alone in the room. There's a suitcase on the floor, he lifts it up to the bed. Sits. Goes to the refrigerator and opens it. There is a naked woman inside.

He gets a bottle of water from the door of the fridge. Drinks from the spout.

FIGURE 2.3 Johnny Shea and Helen Clark in the Cherry Arts production, Ithaca, NY, 2017. The production was lit entirely by practical light fixtures, with the exception of the Woman. When the "refrigerator" was "open," she was bathed in bluish theater light. *Video capture by Al Grunwell.*

SON. He asked about you, you got his attention.

Things like that tend to get attention.

WOMAN. Things like what?

SON. Like your body, I mean you're naked in the refrigerator, it's striking.

WOMAN. You think he's never seen a naked woman?

SON. He asked me about your nudity . . .

WOMAN. How did you answer him?

SON. Evasively . . .

WOMAN. Not that much to say.

SON. No, of course, not much.

WOMAN. He blushed, he closed the door, after a second he opened it again like he was confirming he wasn't hallucinating.

SON. He didn't seem frightened.

WOMAN. Not frightened, excited maybe.

What time is all this?

SON. Pretty late.

WOMAN. Did he come on his own?

SON. I went to pick him up.

I got there a little late.

He was sitting very still.

Sitting on that suitcase.

There on the platform.

He'd got off the bus and I wasn't there.

He was a little nervous, must be why he sat down, calm his nerves.

There were a lot of people, right then he was thinking: I've never been somewhere with so many people.

WOMAN. He said "excuse me," when he opened the door again, he said "excuse me, I didn't know there was anybody else in the apartment."

I started to say, "Nobody knows," but he was already starting to shut the door.

SON. I apologized for being late.

I'd forgotten how punctual he is.

He didn't want us to take the subway, he wanted to see the city.

I told him, you're going to get sick of seeing the city, there's city every-where.

But he insisted, so we took a bus.

WOMAN. He has a picture of you in his wallet.

When you were a newborn. Those pictures they take of babies with their little butts in the air. On a perfectly clean white blanket. Like a little angel.

SON. We got here. He put down the suitcase and I asked him what he wanted to do first.

WOMAN. He was tired this afternoon, he took a nap, and I went through the pockets of his pants at the foot of the bed.

Women pick up these kinds of habits.

I saw your photo.

I recognized you right away.

You haven't changed that much.

SON. Let's go to the zoo, he said. Don't you want to rest? I asked him.

He said, no, I want to make use of the day.

WOMAN. Men undress quickly, and then it seems like they're in a rush to put their clothes back on. Like being naked was uncomfortable. Like they're not used to it. Clothes always itch me. Uncomfortable, tight. Even sheets bother me. Afterwards you have to wash them, wring them out, get out all that dark material running out of them, hang them in the sun, wait for them to dry.

Skin is different, skin you can wash faster.

My skin.

Some people are born without shame, it doesn't bother them to show their skin. Like newborns, they don't know they're being looked at, it's later they're in a rush to cover up.

It's later they learn shame.

SON. I haven't changed that much? Is that what you said?

WOMAN. You look surprised, happens to babies when you take their picture, they make a surprised face. Like the one you just made.

SON. Maybe he wished I'd told him beforehand. I mean, if he saw you this afternoon and let all those hours go by, he was probably waiting for a confession.

WOMAN. You just went kind of pale.

SON. I never imagined having you here either.

I mean, I never put up those posters teenage boys always put up in their rooms, those photos of women with their mouths open.

FIGURE 2.4 Clark, Robinson and Shea in the Cherry Arts production, 2017. The production was in the round, in a small rectangular space with the audience in close proximity on all sides. *Video capture by Al Grunwell.*

WOMAN. I think he smiled, I noticed a kind of smile just as the door was closing.

SON. He made a comment when we were coming here in the bus. I asked him about the trip, how was the trip, just asking . . . he said it rained, a thin rain all night long. Said he couldn't sleep. He doesn't have problems sleeping but he said he was anxious, he looked out the window, the road, the dark. And he said for a second the bus' headlights lit up some of the women who work at night, on the shoulder of the road, to help out the truckers. That's what he said, he saw them for just a second, soaked, shivering in the cold.

SON puts the bottle in the fridge and closes the door. WOMAN stays shut in. FATHER comes out of the bathroom.

FATHER. Sometimes I think about you and I can't believe it.

SON. You're making me uncomfortable.

FATHER. That you've made out so well.

Living in the city and all that.

SON. I always wanted to live here.

FATHER. I like it, but it's overwhelming.

SON. What do you like most?

FATHER. I like the zoo the best.

SON. We can go again if you want, we can go back tomorrow.

FATHER. Oh, today's visit was enough.

It's too bad we didn't see that polar bear.

SON. He's probably dead.

FATHER. That first time, didn't seem you liked the zoo that much.

SON. I liked the elephants. Always.

FATHER. At first you were afraid of them.

SON. Maybe at the beginning—later I couldn't take my eyes off them.

FATHER. And then you wanted to go home, you didn't want to walk around anymore.

SON. After the elephants, nothing else seemed important.

FATHER. They must've been cold that afternoon.

SON. Curling up their trunks, making a hole in the ground.

FATHER. Maybe they weren't cold, maybe they didn't like being seen naked.

SON. They're animals from hot climates. Africa, India, very hot.

FATHER. I'm thirsty, could you get me a glass of water?

SON. I don't have any glasses, you mind drinking out of the bottle?

FATHER. No.

SON. The ones I had broke, no place is open now to get new ones.

FATHER. Don't worry about it. I like drinking out of the bottle—thing is, your mother doesn't like it when I do.

SON. It's not the most hygienic but I'm alone, who'm I going to infect.

FATHER. I'd be a savage too, if it wasn't for your mother.

SON takes the bottle of water out of the fridge and gives it to FATHER, who drinks from the bottle. When he's done he cleans the mouth of the bottle with his sleeve and gives it back. SON also drinks a bit and puts the bottle back in the fridge.

FATHER. Will you be offended if I ask you something?

SON. No, of course not.

FATHER. I was going to ask you if you didn't have desires.

SON. For what?

FATHER. Whenever you open the fridge. Desires for the woman.

SON. It never occurred to me. Why do you ask?

FATHER. Just to ask, that's all.

SON. You?

FATHER. Me what?

SON. What happened to you when you saw her.

FATHER. The first thing that got my attention is that she didn't have any marks from a bra, I don't know if you noticed.

SON. No, I didn't.

FATHER. It must be I'm so used to your mother—on her back, when she takes off her blouse at night, it's like her bra divides her back into two sections, I don't know if you noticed.

SON. No, I haven't seen her in a long time.

FATHER. It didn't use to be like that, it was like her back was one single thing. Over time it separated. I think the bra was what did it.

SON. I'm not interested in the subject.

FATHER. When she puts on her nightgown and takes it off, it leaves like a red bar. Sometimes she puts cream on it. You know? Sometimes, the heat, the sweat, the skin.

SON. I don't want to imagine it.

FIGURE 2.5 Robinson, Shea, and Clark in the Cherry Arts production, 2017. *Video capture by Al Grunwell.*

FATHER. The first time I saw your mother naked was the night we were married. I'm sure that'll make you laugh but that's the way it was. She pulled the sheets over herself and I turned on the light, pulled back the sheet and looked at her. She covered her eyes with her hands. To not look at me look at her. She was always ashamed to be naked. She asked me to please turn out the light, I could do what I wanted but in the dark.

Some light came in the window. The hotel was called The Danube. It was the only one in town. It was at the side of the highway, where the roadhouse is now.

We didn't do anything that night, I don't know if you understand . . .

SON. I think I understand.

FATHER. She was very nervous, and me too. She was shaking. I hugged her to warm her up.

Are you cold? I asked her.

She calmed down, little by little.

You can't imagine how soft her skin was.

I've never seen a woman more naked than she was that night.

SON. I'm not interested in imagining.

FATHER. I squeezed her tight. Very tight. And right there I felt her naked body was a talisman.

The nude of all nudes.

From then on, all other bodies would be the same body. Sometimes when I close my eyes I find it all over again.

When I search for my talisman with my eyes squeezed shut.

SON. What does that have to do with what you were saying about the woman and the fridge.

FATHER. I went off on a tangent . . . I wanted to say that the woman in the fridge didn't have any marks, like she'd never worn a bra.

Like the girls in the roadhouse by the highway, I don't know where they got them from, skin like . . . later, I mean, in time the quality went down, they had older girls, or maybe the same girls but they'd gotten older.

Got old I should say. Skin gets rough, like leather.

But what am I talking to you about, you're an intellectual, what's all this going to matter to you, girls and bras.

Do you read at night or watch television?

I'm asking so I don't bother you.

SON. Depends. Some nights I read, some nights I watch TV.

FATHER. When I opened the door, her skin was prickly, what's that called?

SON. Goosebumps.

FATHER. That, her skin was like that.

Her nipples were erect, hard like, it doesn't bother you I said nipples? I'd never say that word in front of your mother. She wouldn't say so but she'd think it was common, to say nipple.

SON. It doesn't bother me. I believe it happens from the cold.

FATHER. To us too, that part of the body shows /the cold . . .

SON. Yeah, it happens . . .

FATHER. End of the day, there's all kinds of people, even people who live in the fridge.

You wouldn't think there could be that type of life.

Shut in, ice and humidity.

SON. I think the humidity is good for her skin.

FATHER. Yeah, her skin was beautiful.

SON. Moisturizes the skin . . .

FATHER. I'm gonna lie down.

Then let's watch television. [If it] Doesn't bother you, sometimes it's nice to not think.

FATHER takes off his pants, folds them carefully, and puts them on the suitcase. SON turns on the TV. FATHER watches. SON takes off his pants and leaves them where they fall on the floor. He takes off his T-shirt, lies on the bed beside FATHER. They both watch in silence.

FATHER. Would you mind making me a coffee?

SON. Will you be able to sleep if you drink coffee this late?

FATHER. Coffee doesn't even make me yawn.

SON. I have instant, I can put milk in if you want.

FATHER. OK, if you feel like it, put milk in.

SON. Then I'll put milk in.

FATHER. If you have anything stronger, put a little in.

SON. Like what?

FATHER. Gin or something.

SON. No, I don't have any, I can go get some if you want.

FATHER. No, no, I don't want any, it was to make the coffee stronger, that's all.

SON puts the water on. Approaches FATHER. Sits at his side, they watch the TV.

45

WINTER ANIMALS

FATHER. It's a bit chilly.

SON. The coffee will help.

FATHER. Yes, I'll be fine with the coffee.

SON. Want me to make you a hot water bottle?

FATHER. I don't want to put you out.

SON. It's no bother—we can take advantage of the water that's heating.

FATHER. Naw, don't make one. A little cold is good.

SON. Don't get yourself sick.

FATHER. On the contrary. It's good for the circulation.

SON. What?

FATHER. Your blood. Flows better in the cold. That's why the girl has that skin, you can see her blood circulating through it, you know?

SON. You take it with sugar.

FATHER. No, black.

SON. I have sugar.

FATHER. Those aspirins, I take one every day. For my circulation.

SON. I have Sweet 'n' Low if you want.

FATHER. You're . . . on a diet?

SON. No. I got it cause some people don't take sugar.

FATHER. Who?

SON. People . . .

FATHER. But you live here and you take sugar. Didn't you say nobody ever comes here?

SON. I thought if one day someone came, they might want it with Sweet 'n' Low . . . actually I didn't even think that, one day I just bought Sweet 'n' Low . . .

FATHER. Before long you're going to have to start taking an aspirin every day.

SON. Even though I feel fine?

FATHER. Better to start taking them before you get sick. Preventative.

SON prepares the coffee and serves it. FATHER drinks. Another silence.

FATHER. Do you have a bit of bread left?

SON. I think there's a little. You want it?

FATHER. If you're not gonna, it's better to eat it before it gets hard.

SON serves bread. FATHER breaks it, dunks the chunk in the coffee, eats it. SON watches.

SON. Is it good?

FATHER. Yeah. I like ground coffee better, but instant isn't bad. You're not having any?

SON. I don't drink it this late.

FATHER. There's good coffee in this city.

SON. I'm not an expert.

FATHER. But coffee is good, I like it. Geez, wasn't that great coffee we had this afternoon?

SON. Yeah, it was great.

FATHER. There's only one bar back there and the coffee always tastes burned. I only found out by comparing. I'm used to the taste, but then I got here and realized how crappy that coffee is.

SON. You could drink something else. Order something other than coffee.

FATHER. I could, but sometimes you feel like drinking coffee, no matter how terrible it is. The first time we came here, you were little, but I couldn't stop drinking coffee. You had hot cocoa.

You liked that word, cocoa . . .

SON. I still like it.

FATHER. That trip, that first trip, after the zoo we went to the movies.

SON. To see *The Ten Commandments* in Cinerama.

FIGURE 2.6 Clark, Robinson, and Shea in the Cherry Arts production, 2017. *Photograph by Samuel Buggeln.*

FATHER. Like I was seeing it now. Moses traversing the desert, leading his people.

And that scene with the sea, when they had to cross the sea . . . a terrible, raging sea . . .

SON. I was scared, I was scared in that scene.

FATHER. Moses before his people. With a stick, like a staff touching the water. That moment, you grabbed my hand, and the waters parted.

A path down the middle of the sea, between two thick walls of water, and the people traversing.

SON. "Traverse the great waters" . . . that's a phrase from the I-Ching. I've been thinking about that for days now.

FATHER. About what?

SON. About the sea opening. Getting out of here, going far away, to another continent.

FATHER. Go even further away?

SON. Live on the other side.

Another life.

FATHER. When people start running away, they can't stop.

Think of the flight of the Jews out of Egypt, they couldn't ever stop.

It's good to put down roots, stay still.

SON. All this unpeacefulness . . .

If I stay here much longer, I could explode into a million pieces.

FATHER. I can't concentrate.

SON. I guess that's what the TV's for. Stop people concentrating.

FATHER. We could turn up the volume.

SON. I try not to turn up the volume this late. They already came by to complain.

FATHER. Don't you need a plant in this apartment?

SON. What for?

FATHER. Something that'd have a bit of life.

SON. I don't need that.

FATHER. Your mother could give you a cutting of something.

You have no idea how beautiful they are! Some of them look like plastic, they're that pretty.

SON. I don't want anything alive. It'd put me out.

FATHER. She has a little palm tree, you have no idea how she keeps it up!

They don't have palm trees like that in the Caribbean.

SON. I'm not good with plants.

FATHER. You know what, you're going to find out if you're good when you have a plant.

SON. That's not how it works. At least not for me.

FATHER. She talks to them, you have no idea, she talks to them like crazy!

SON. What does she talk about?

FATHER. Sometimes she prays to them.

SON. Things people do . . .

FATHER. So funny! She talks more to that palm tree than she does to me!

SON. Should we turn off the television?

FATHER. You have no idea how she loves that palm tree!

It's in the entryway, in the garden, you must have seen it.

SON. No, I haven't seen it.

FATHER. You didn't pay attention, but you've definitely seen it.

It's the envy of all the neighbors.

They say, how does she manage to have a palm tree like that, in this climate.

Those palm trees do better in the tropics, in the Caribbean, places like that . . .

SON. I haven't seen it.

FATHER. Because it's been so long since you've been there.

SON. Next time I'll pay attention.

FATHER. Nah you won't.

None of that stuff is important to you.

SON. . . .

SON turns off the television.

FATHER. I mean about the neighbors and what they envy.

You never cared what they thought.

You don't care what other people think.

SON. I dunno, could be.

FATHER. In the city, they think small-town people are good people, and it's not true.

Small town people are evil, they are evil.

FIGURE 2.7 Shanly in the Elefante production, Buenos Aires, 2011. *Photograph by Nora Lezano.*

SON. I'm not sure it's any better here.

FATHER. Least you never find out what people think.

Out there it's so small you can practically hear people's thoughts.

SON. Maybe, I'm not sure.

I don't know what city people are like, I still don't know.

FATHER. You haven't met anyone?

I mean have you met anyone you care about, I mean have you made relationships, like affections, connections.

SON. Just passing acquaintanceships.

Nothing important.

FATHER. But you don't have any friends?

SON. Friends. The thing they call friends I do not have.

FATHER. I thought you left to make friends.

SON. No, that's not why I left.

FATHER. So why did you leave?

SON. Just . . . to leave.

FATHER. You seemed sort of alone, so I thought . . .

SON. What was going to keep me there?

FATHER. That's what I always said to your mother, what's going to keep him here . . . ?

SON. What did she say?

FATHER. She said some kinds of sons stay with their mothers.

SON. Stay how long?

FATHER. Stay forever.

She feels betrayed.

SON. By what? By who?

FATHER. I'm just guessing.

That she feels betrayed you left.

I'm saying it's hard for parents to watch a son grow up.

SON. She didn't say anything, when she came she didn't say anything to me.

FATHER. That's how she speaks, by not saying anything, being silent.

I'm accustomed to her being silent.

But you don't have to worry about your parents, we're good, you have to do the things guys do when they come to the city.

Adapt.

SON. What things.

FATHER. Well . . . go out dancing.

You could go out dancing.

SON. What for?

FATHER. I don't know, why do, why do young people go out dancing. Meet a girl, for example.

SON. I don't feel like meeting anyone.

FATHER. I can understand that.

At your age I didn't want to meet anyone either, but one day I met your mother and you know the rest of the story.

SON. I do know it.

FATHER. Now I can't imagine myself being alone.

Can't imagine it.

Before, sure.

My stomach hurts a bit.

SON. I can't imagine you alone either.

Can't see it.

FATHER. I liked being alone in the country.

When my father would send me out to bring down the cattle . . .

Going on my own, traversing all that distance.

Alone.

I'd cross the river, wait for the cows to drink something.

I liked to take off my clothes and get in the river while I was waiting.

I mean who could see me, naked in the sun while the cows drank water and the horse munched on the grass.

At the time I didn't know it, but that—lying out there naked—that's what they call freedom.

SON. I can't imagine you.

FATHER. What do you mean you can't imagine. I was the same as you: a wild animal.

My body even looked like yours.

SON. There are things sons can't imagine about their fathers.

FATHER. Because for you I've always had this body, but I haven't. Fathers watch their children grow up, but children don't see their fathers grow up. I had a very flexible body, very skinny.

I'm sure when you're alone, I mean here, you go around naked too.

SON. Maybe, I don't notice—or I don't do it on purpose.

FATHER. That's what I mean, when you're naked without realizing you're naked, you understand?

SON. OK, I understand.

FATHER. Like the woman who lives in your fridge.

She's that kind of person.

What're they called? Nudists, that's her kind of nakedness.

Folks who don't even notice they're not wearing clothes. Mean no harm—naked just because.

Naked to be naked, no other reason, not trying to say anything with the naked body: simply naked.

SON. You're sweating.

FATHER. I have a stitch in my stomach, like something disagreed with me.

I think it's the coffee.

If your mother doesn't let me drink coffee this late, she must have a reason.

Do you have a glass of Coca Cola? That's good for the stomach.

SON. I do, but that has more caffeine, I don't think it'll be good for you.

FATHER. If caffeine disagrees with you, it's best to have a little more.

Like alcohol, the day after you get drunk. Have a drink of alcohol on an empty stomach, you get rid of the hangover. That's a man's secret.

SON. I have a little Coke, I don't know if it still has fizz.

FATHER. I'd take a little glass.

SON. I'll put it in a coffee cup, I don't have glasses remember, we can buy a couple tomorrow.

FATHER. Sure, doesn't change the taste.

I mean who's watching us, we can drink out of whatever we want!

SON opens the door of the fridge, WOMAN extends her hand with a mug of coke. SON grabs it and gives it to FATHER, who drinks.

FATHER. It must be surprising to people, you're so polite.

SON. I don't see why they'd be surprised.

FATHER. Well, you're so nice.

People here are hard, they don't have time to be nice.

People from the country are friendly. They're evil, but they're friendly.

SON. . . .

FATHER. You hear that? You used to like that sound. See, it still had fizz! . . . You used to like to hear the sound of the bubbles in the soda popping on the surface.

You said it was like listening to sparks popping in the fire.

The same sound but inverted.

Invert.

I never liked that word.

I prefer homo.

You know I never met a homo? I've seen them on TV, like everybody, but I've never met one.

They say the schoolteacher in town . . . well, they like to run their mouths in that town, but they say that's why he killed himself, they say because he was a homo.

SON. Are you feeling better?

FATHER. A little.

Put your hand here, on my belly.

You hear it?

SON. No, but I feel it.

FATHER. It's my guts complaining.

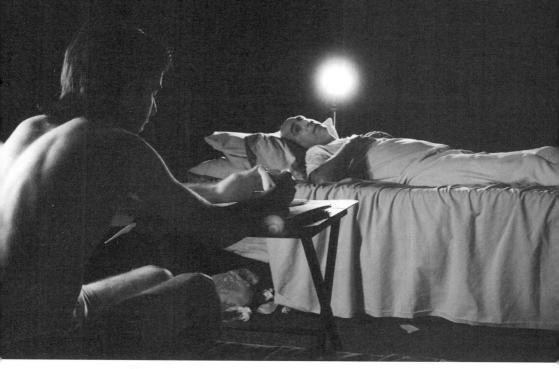

FIGURE 2.8 Shea and Robinson in the Cherry Arts production, 2017. *Photograph by Samuel Buggeln.*

Around now they almost always do, sometimes they make more noise.

So much noise your mother says it wakes her up.

That's why she prefers to sleep in the living room. Because of my noisy guts.

SON. It'd be better if you laid down.

FATHER. What was I saying?

Oh yes, about being alone . . . well, if I'd never met your mother, you wouldn't be here.

And just like I'm saying it to you, in some future, you could say the same to your son. I mean, anything can happen.

SON. Of course, anything.

FATHER. The day you were born I knew real happiness. I'm telling you so you know.

It embarrasses you to hear that.

You just made the same gesture people made that day.

You lowered your eyes.

When you were born, I realized that happiness produces a kind of embarrassment in people.

It's not easy to hear someone's happy. The opposite is bearable, but happiness makes people uncomfortable, could be because it leaves so quickly, or because it doesn't happen often. I don't know.

I realized that day that my happiness made other people uncomfortable.

That must be it, the discomfort, or the embarrassment, that must be why happiness doesn't come back.

SON pulls out a small folding table out from beside the fridge. He sets it up and places a chair in front, improvising a writing desk. He puts some cardboard boxes on the table and takes out a pile of forms. He sits and carefully fills out the forms.

FATHER. You're going to work this late?

SON. I barely got anything done today, it'd be good if I did some work, even a few minutes.

FATHER. It's good to be able to work in your own house, and whenever you want to, I always would've liked that.

SON. Yeah, it's good.

FATHER. And it can't be very complicated, I mean you don't have to think too much.

SON. No, you don't need to think much. Just complete the information, make things up, fill the blanks.

FATHER. I thought they had computers for that kind of thing.

SON. Not yet, not for making things up—plus these surveys have to be filled out by hand.

FATHER. You were always fast at that kind of work, fast and organized.

SON. I don't mind it.

I can think about other things while I do it.

FATHER. And to not have to go out to work, take buses, walk in the street, all that craziness.

SON. I'm kind of cheating. I should be going to houses and asking, but I prefer to stay here and do them myself. So far I'm getting away with it.

FATHER. Sometimes a bit of cheating is OK.

SON. I go days without going out. It's better.

FATHER. Sure, it's better not to go out.

If I could, I wouldn't go out.

SON. Plus I invent things, put stuff down.

Some of these surveys are really bad, so I exaggerate.

Here, where they ask about the children's education, you see?

Here, for the ages, I give them ridiculous ages, or for example I gave this family two extra kids. Or when they ask about the house, for "type of domicile" I always put "luxurious," even though from the other answers I'm guessing they live in a shack.

I do that so they don't have problems—sometimes these surveys are for credit card applications. Just imagine the happiness, when the credit card arrives down there at the shack.

FATHER. Just imagine! That's funny.

SON. By completing these surveys, I complete their lives.

FATHER. How great to feel useful, I would have liked that.

Plus, you're doing your thing, right?

To be able to do your thing.

Do what you wanted to do.

SON. And what did I want to do?

FATHER. You wanted to get out of that town and dedicate yourself to writing.

As a kid you read a lot, wrote in secret.

Who would've thought you'd end up in the city, writing.

SON. Sure . . .

FATHER. That's what's important, being consistent.

Persevering.

And knowing what you're persevering for, "persevere and triumph"—but staying clear about what for, I mean if you persevere and don't know what for . . .

Something like that happened to me, getting up every morning . . .

SON. . . .

FATHER. I could see you were sad in that town. Like you'd outgrown it.

That's why you wrote sad things.

I can see you're better now. When we met each other this morning, I could see you were doing better . . .

SON. . . .

FATHER. A time is going to come when there won't be any sadness. Not one single kind of sadness: a long, long time . . .

Ever since you were little, I knew you were destined for great things.

SON. What things?

FATHER. I don't know what things but I'm sure they're great.

There are things we don't even understand yet.

At the present they can't be understood.

SON. What things are you talking about?

FATHER. Things in general.

Everything . . .

SON isn't listening, he's absorbed in the surveys and doesn't answer. FATHER turns over toward the wall. He covers himself and stays quiet.

SON picks up the mug. Drinks the last sip of Coke. Puts the mug on the floor.

WOMAN comes out of the fridge. She sits next to SON.

WOMAN. Is he asleep?

SON. He sleeps easily.

WOMAN. I'm going to show you the photo from his pocket.

SON. As long as he doesn't wake up.

WOMAN. He has a talent for sleep.

SON. Not a quality I inherited.

WOMAN. Look at the picture.

Look at him sleep.

Little angel.

Are you nervous?

SON. Insomnia. Recurring nightmares.

WOMAN. Do you want me to relax you?

SON. I can do it myself.

WOMAN. Look how skinny you are.

SON. I've turned into a nocturnal animal.

WOMAN. I can count your ribs, one after the other.

Not his, he has some fat.

SON. Even back then I didn't sleep.

I had to go to school and it kept me up all night.

Walking around the house.

That's why I started to read, to pass the night more quickly.

WOMAN. He has rough skin, not like yours, yours is like a sheet.

Like you barely had skin.

A thin sheet that's about to be cut.

SON. One night I couldn't sleep, I forced the drawer of his desk.

The drawer he'd forbidden me to open.

WOMAN. Are you scared? Don't worry.

Everyone has fear, even if they pretend not to.

SON. There were letters in the drawer. Correspondence.

I started to read them but there wasn't much light.

Between the envelopes I found a pen.

It was quite thick, definitely imported. Divided in half.

WOMAN. I think he's murmuring something in his sleep.

He's barely moving his mouth—sounds are coming out.

I can't tell what he's saying.

It's dry out here, I always feel like I'm suffocating.

SON. The bottom part was opaque, and the top was transparent. With clear liquid and the figure of a little woman.

A blonde woman, I remember she was blonde.

Wearing a little suit like a secretary—I remember I thought, she must be a secretary; and then I turned over the pen and the little suit went up in smoke and there was the blonde woman, naked.

Right there, teeny and naked and me not knowing what to do, embarrassed in the middle of the night, no idea what to do with this naked woman inside the pen.

And I thought, if I take this to school, everybody will admire me and the boys will want to be around me, so I closed the drawer and took the pen with me to bed.

WOMAN. I'm afraid you're going to break.

Like if I hug you, you could crack into pieces.

I've never held such a fragile body.

Doesn't seem to bother you that I use the word fragile.

Bothers other men.

FIGURE 2.9 (FACING PAGE) Martin Shanly and Valeria Roldán in the Elefante production, Buenos Aires, 2011. *Photograph by Nora Lezano.*

Not you.

Your body is almost a woman's.

SON. But the next day. When I saw the pen in the light of the day, between the sheets, I felt a little disgusted.

I can't explain.

Like something bad had happened, a crime or something.

I mean something too bad to even talk about after.

So I threw the pen in a vacant lot on the way to school.

There was a lime pit and I threw it and buried it in the lime with a stick . . . it disappeared in the whiteness of the lime.

WOMAN. I feel comfortable with you.

Your body doesn't feel dangerous.

WOMAN caresses SON's face. He closes his eyes as if he hadn't noticed the caress.

WOMAN. I am the woman.

I'm between two men.

This is the story.

A father and a son.

And I'm the woman.

If I'm here, it's for a reason.

The connection of fathers to sons.

The line of continuity.

Descendence.

I'm dewy, and naked.

And I'm here to hear you.

SON. What should I say?

WOMAN. The kind of thing I'd have to be here for, the things you whisper . . .

SON. I feel dizzy, that same sensation . . .

WOMAN. It's happened before, the same dizziness . . .

SON. Yes, it has—the sleeplessness too, it'll keep happening, long after, years later.

WOMAN. Sometimes sleep can come—when you sleep with someone else the other can pull you into sleep . . .

SON. It won't be like that, the insomnia will keep on. I'll pass a few nights contemplating the world where others sleep.

The insomnia will keep leaving marks below my eyes, on my skin.

WOMAN. Skin needs to rest too.

SON. Of course, skin too.

It was after the thing with the pen, just before I started to mature.

The thing with the skin . . .

WOMAN. What thing?

SON. Looking at my skin in the mirror, every day looking at my skin.

I'd heard the illness started on the skin.

After that I'd lock myself in the bathroom and search for stains on my skin.

You heard about it, pink marks on the skin that appeared on homosexuals.

I'd never slept with anyone, I mean I'd barely stopped being a child and a couple of kids at school called me a faggot, that's it, nothing to take seriously.

And then I heard about the pink plague.

And I was afraid the stains would appear and confirm what the school kids were saying.

WOMAN. It's frightening, to confirm something.

SON. Unbearable fear. Insomnia.

The fear of going to sleep and not being able to wake up.

Not wanting to die, not wanting the opposite.

Go to the bathroom, take off my clothes, examine my skin again and again.

All my skin, my entire skin.

Stay locked in my room.

Conduct an entirely private life.

WOMAN. You mean never go out?

SON. Of course, no, never.

An animal isn't just an animal, it's also his cage.

WOMAN. Don't be afraid. You're going to live many years. Enough years to forget everything.

SON. Everything?

WOMAN. Even sleep, and the lack of it. Even the nightmares, you'll even lose that memory.

SON. And I'll have a body like his . . .

WOMAN. Of course, a body like that.

SON. I'm watching him sleep now.

This is the image I'll remember of him.

This calm way of sleeping.

This will all be remembered.

WOMAN. I'm drying out.

And I lived afloat, in a long dream.

SON. Like an astronaut in liquid.

WOMAN. Wet, completely wet . . .

SON. . . . that's why I should've left the pen in the drawer . . . Mom knew he kept women on the side . . . to feel less alone in those moments . . . and when he'd been looking for you for a couple of days, he asked me: are you sure you didn't open the drawer in the desk? No, I told him, I'm sure I didn't open it . . . and later the woman by the road . . . all that skin . . . the perfume of the skin . . . he's probably dreaming of all

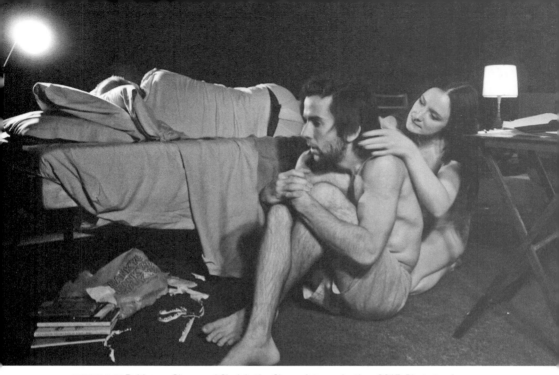

FIGURE 2.10 Robinson, Shea, and Clark in the Cherry Arts production, 2017. *Photograph by Samuel Buggeln.*

that skin . . . with you, by the road, with the neon light that paints you as he gestures . . . and you turn nude . . .

WOMAN. Whatever he's dreaming, he's calm.

SON. He sleeps and I watch him and all this will be remembered, all of it, with details and forgettings.

You there asleep while I'm so wakeful.

If you embraced me I could sleep.

If I could be close to your body and embrace you and attach myself to your sleep . . .

. . . the same story over and over . . . of the son who can't embrace his father . . . the father who can't embrace his son . . .

WOMAN returns to the refrigerator and closes herself in. FATHER wakes and sits up in bed. He looks at SON.

FATHER. I must be feeling relaxed right now, 'cause I forgot to brush my teeth.

SON. It's chilly. If you get up undressed, your tummy won't get better.

FATHER. I wasn't thinking about brushing my teeth, it was just to say it. I noticed I'd forgotten.

SON. You don't wash, you don't brush your teeth, wait 'til Mom finds out about all this.

FATHER. It can be our secret.

Plus I didn't bring a toothbrush.

SON. You could use mine if you want.

FATHER. It wouldn't bother you. [?]

All those germs.

SON. It wouldn't bother me, I'm sure my mouth has germs too.

FATHER. They say you shouldn't share . . . you shouldn't share intimate stuff, you can catch something.

SON. I'm not sick.

FATHER. Sometimes my gums bleed a little when I brush my teeth.

SON. That's not contagious.

FATHER. I end up with the taste of blood in my mouth, I can taste it during the day.

Blood and mint.

A salty taste.

SON. You should have that looked at.

FATHER. It's normal.

They say at a certain age, things like that start to happen.

SON. Maybe it's the aspirins, they thin the blood, it might be the aspirins you take.

FATHER. Could be, everything that does good also does evil, they say, everything's basically relative.

Why don't you go to bed?

SON. I can't sleep.

FATHER. Red!

SON. What?

FATHER. The sea the Jews traversed in the movie was red.

SON. Where did that come from?

FATHER. I just remembered, even the screen looked red.

The first time I heard that I thought it was because of the blood.

SON. What blood?

FATHER. When the Jews are finished crossing the sea, remember the Pharaoh's troops pursue them in their flight.

And at the end, when the people have crossed.

When Moses is sure all his people are safe.

He touches the path that he had made in the water with his staff and the seas closes, the water falls on the pharaoh's troops and they all die, drowned in the sea, that must be why it's red.

SON. I'm not sure drowned people bleed, they swell up but they don't bleed.

FATHER. You're always thinking so much . . .

Are you cold?

SON. The usual.

FATHER. I couldn't sleep either, keeping a woman in the refrigerator.

SON. We're not going to talk about that, not this late.

FATHER. I was thinking we could put the beds together.

Make a double bed. I mean . . .

SON. It's very late.

FATHER. And her in the middle. Making a balance between the two beds, it'd be fun.

SON. Doesn't sound fun to me.

FATHER. Always so serious.

As if that woman didn't have her charms!

She was even checking me out, I'm sure she checked me out!

You know what that woman's missing? A man.

That man is here!

A man has come to this house!

SON. Lower your voice!

Everyone can hear you.

FATHER. Why, are you embarrassed?

We're among men, we're men.

We have the confidence to say that kind of thing.

SON. Please lower the volume of your voice.

There are neighbors, people are sleeping.

FATHER. Let them wake up!

Let 'em all wake up!

'Cause a man has come, a man from the land!

An animal from the land!

A wild animal, a beast!

SON. That's enough! I got the idea, loud and clear, now calm down.

Lie down before you get cold.

FATHER. It doesn't hurt, to sleep with someone else.

SON. I'm accustomed to sleeping alone.

FATHER. . . . You're talking about me being here.

SON. It was a comment, nothing more.

FATHER. You can say it.

I already know.

Even at the zoo you were uncomfortable.

SON. A simple comment that I didn't expect to produce a lot of consequences.

FATHER. I bought a double bag of popcorn and you didn't want to try any.

SON. I didn't feel like it.

FATHER. I ate the whole bag and after I didn't have an appetite for dinner, that's why I'm hungry now.

SON. You don't understand not feeling like something, not having desires, same thing, no desire to eat popcorn.

FATHER. I understand what I understand.

I'm old but I can still understand a few things.

SON. Then try to understand this—my not feeling like eating popcorn is not a phenomenon that is directed at you.

FATHER. Don't try to drown me with words.

You've always been so arrogant.

Your mother used to say that, that boy and his arrogant silence.

SON. It's late, let's not argue.

FATHER. Even as a boy you'd stare at us in silence.

This superior silence.

SON. Where is all this coming from. I'm lost.

FATHER. The fact you've read a few more books doesn't make you more intelligent.

SON. I need to get some air.

FATHER. Yes, I noticed, when I was drinking the coffee.

When I dipped the bread in my coffee, how you looked at me with disgust.

FATHER stands up, moves to the little table and knocks the pile of surveys to the floor. SON leaps up and tries to organize them.

SON. Look what you did, you mixed them all up, now I don't know what order they were in!

FATHER. Such a fuss, I don't see what all the fuss is about . . . in the end, everyone's always [doing the wrong thing] . . . I barely mentioned that woman, as if a father couldn't worry about his son's life.

As if it was easy to come to your son's house, discover there's a woman in the fridge and shut up about it, say everything's fine and chat about this and that.

SON. I already told you, I didn't know her.

She was here when I arrived.

FATHER. Didn't know her? You know her.

Was here—has she left? [naw . . .]

Where could she go if the door is closed?

Did she go while I was asleep?

SON. No. She's still here.

FATHER. Isn't she cold? Too cold?

I mean I could warm her up, it wouldn't bother me.

Maybe she's shivering, her lips, the rest of her body.

SON. She's a bit chilly, but that's her habitat.

FATHER. The fridge?

SON. The place she lives, what she needs to keep her skin hydrated.

FATHER. Doesn't matter to you?

SON. I'm used to it, she has her life and I have mine.

Every so often we say something to each other, but sometimes a number of days go by, I even forget.

FATHER. I can understand that.

Don't be offended, but sometimes I forget about you.

Sometimes I'm even surprised when people ask me about my son.

As if for a moment I said to myself, what son?

I'm so young, when did this "son" thing happen?

What is this thing, having a son?

Sometimes you forget everything that's happened.

SON. Must be something like that with me and the woman and the fridge.

FATHER. It'd be good if you slept now.

SON. I'm not sleepy yet.

FATHER. I'm going to try to sleep a bit more, if it doesn't bother you.

SON. Why would it bother me?

FATHER. Sometimes insomniacs need company.

SON. Not in my case.

> *FATHER turns his body toward the wall, turning his back to SON. SON goes to the fridge and opens it, WOMAN extends her arms. The son hugs her and helps her to get out.*

SON. You were a topic of some dispute.

WOMAN. Two men fighting over me.

It's a compliment.

SON. He's asleep now. Went back to sleep.

WOMAN. Your father is a melancholy animal.

SON. What must he be dreaming of?

WOMAN. Animals.

SON. That was the last time he came.

The first and last time he visited me.

And tomorrow, before he goes, we'll go back to the zoo.

It'll be a cloudy, cold day.

WOMAN. He's dreaming of animals that don't exist.

Animals without cages.

Animals of water and fire.

Planetary animals, animals that float and melt away in the air.

He's dreaming of animals you can see right through.

SON. When we get to the zoo it'll start to drizzle.

FIGURE 2.11 Robinson, Clark, and Shea in the Cherry Arts production, 2017. *Photograph by Samuel Buggeln.*

That winter drizzle that gets through your clothes without your noticing.

The paths between the cages will be empty.

There won't be anybody around.

The animals hiding in their caves and the two of us, walking silently in the flickering water.

The rest, for years to come I won't remember any of it.

. . .

It's like the sea closing the waters after the passage of the Jews.

That's what the memory of this day will be like.

The day my father came to visit.

I was very young, I still had this body.

A long time later, I rescue this moment from the depths of the ocean.

Trapped in that abyss among the rocks and moss.

That sea closed the way wounds heal, so we can keep living.

That's what forgetting is.

Father, tonight I throw you into oblivion.

Father, I'm leaving you here.

I need to keep moving, to go far away.

WOMAN goes into the fridge, leaving the door open. SON lies down next to FATHER, who wakes up.

FATHER. It's weird—for a second I didn't know where I was, I opened my eyes and saw this wall and didn't know it.

SON. I know that feeling, it happened to me at first.

FATHER. That's why it's good to be home, know where you are when you wake up.

SON. Just pretend you're in your house.

FATHER. Sometimes, if you don't know the place, it's like everything is a dream, like there's no division between sleeping and being awake.

SON. It's OK, you're here.

I'm your son and we spent the day together, we went to the zoo, we saw elephants and cages.

FATHER. Yeah, I calmed down as soon as I saw you.

I said, I'm at my son's, in the city, at night and it was as if something inside returned, came close.

SON. Close to where?

FATHER. I don't know to where—close.

SON. My eyes are burning.

FATHER. I think about you a lot. You know?

Forget what I told you before.

The thing about forgetting you sometimes. It's not true.

I remember you even when I've forgot you.

I would've liked to have given you more. At least to know what you needed.

Your mom thinks about you too, she doesn't mention you but I know she thinks about you.

SON. I know that. Thanks.

FATHER. And when you want to talk, whatever you want to talk about, you can talk, and I'll listen, always.

SON. I don't have anything specific to say.

FATHER. Well that's the nice thing, we can also stay quiet.

SON. I go whole days in silence.

Without talking to anyone—suddenly, in the street, I hear my own voice and for a moment it seems foreign—then I get used to it.

FATHER. Happens to all of us.

SON. Sometimes I don't have anything to say.

FATHER. You don't have to say anything.

SON. I have no opinion.

FATHER. Shh shh, quiet.

SON. . . .

FATHER. That's no way to get to sleep.

SON. I'll sleep tomorrow, after you've gone.

FATHER. You need to sleep, if you don't sleep you can't think right.

SON. I'm used to lack of sleep.

FATHER. You have to try.

SON. My whole body is so tired and sleep is nowhere, nowhere.

FATHER. How can you be so tired, so young?

SON. Maybe I'm tired out from the things that are still to happen.

FATHER. Lie down, first you lie down and then sleep comes.

SON. That night you took me to the place with the girls, by the road.

FATHER. I barely remember.

SON. You took me there the same way you took me to school.

FATHER. Don't keep thinking about it, you won't sleep.

SON. When one of the girls took my hand, you made a gesture to her I didn't understand, a gesture I'd never seen, a gesture you'd never made to Mom.

FATHER. By the way, what time is it?

SON. Complicity, that was the gesture.

After the gesture you kissed me on the forehead.

Like when you left me at the door to the school.

FATHER. Children look for significance where there isn't any, parents do stupid things—that won't happen to you, you won't have children.

SON. I'd fallen asleep . . .

FATHER. Come, lie on my chest.

SON. Now suddenly sleep is coming.

FATHER. Here, lying on my body.

Nothing bad is going to happen.

SON. In this place, where I'm sleeping.

FATHER. Shhhh.

I'm with you.

SON. You're my father, we spent the day together.

Tomorrow we'll go to the zoo together for the last time.

It's already nighttime.

Past nighttime, dawn.

FATHER. Feel how my stomach goes up and down, with every breath.

SON. The heart.

The beating.

I'm asleep.

FIGURE 2.12 Félix, Shanly, and Roldán in the Elefante production, Buenos Aires, 2011. *Photograph by Nora Lezano.*

SON sleeps. They remain embraced. WOMAN has stayed still in the refrigerator up to this moment. Now she moves, looks toward FATHER who continues embracing his son, as if cradling him.

FATHER. He's asleep.

He's finally asleep.

WOMAN. I listen to him pacing around all night long like he was in a cage.

FATHER. He's always been anxious.

Abstracted, and anxious.

WOMAN. He's resting now.

FATHER. I'm happy you're here.

Though I have to admit you excite me a little.

WOMAN. Should I take that as a compliment?

FATHER. A fact. When I saw you I felt excited, like I used to feel years ago.

WOMAN. Thanks.

FATHER. I should be thanking you.

You're near my son.

Even if only in that refrigerator.

A man should have a woman nearby.

WOMAN. You think so?

FATHER. I was raised to think that kind of thing.

It worries me, this kid is so alone.

WOMAN. Are you worried he's going to turn out weird?

FATHER. No.

WOMAN. . . . ?

FATHER. I'm worried he's going to turn out sad.

WOMAN. That is inevitable.

FATHER. I don't want it to happen.

I mean, I don't want anything bad to happen to him.

WOMAN. It is inevitable.

FATHER. I like watching him sleep.

WOMAN. When men sleep they become tame animals.

FATHER. He sleeps so little—it's like he's denying me the pleasure.

Of watching him sleep.

He looks so big to me.

I see him and I don't recognize him.

Only when he's asleep.

Then he's the same as always.

WOMAN. I'm sure that little cubby is going to have a good life.

FATHER. Do you think so?

WOMAN. Of course.

A good life and a long one.

FATHER. It's doing him good to rest.

Tomorrow he'll wake up a little less sad.

WOMAN. Are you going to come back to visit him?

FATHER. Of course, how could I not come back?

WOMAN. He needs people to come back.

FATHER. I'm the type of person who comes back.

I always come back.

WOMAN. I'm a little chilly.

FATHER. Later we'll make room for you.

Here in the middle.

WOMAN. Thanks.

FATHER. Right now I'm afraid he'd wake up.

I'm afraid if I move him, no more sleep.

WOMAN. Don't move him.

FATHER. His breath is slow . . .

WOMAN. Don't move him.

FATHER. . . . .

WOMAN. Let him get some more sleep.

FATHER. I'm falling asleep too . . .

. . . little by little . . . I'm falling asleep . . .

. . . I'm going to sleep . . .

THE END

TRANSLATOR/EDITOR'S NOTE

My perspective on *Winter Animals* is deeply informed by the fact that it is the first play I directed while also being a co-author of the translation. (In 2017, the Cherry Artists' Collective produced the play in a double bill with *Nothing to Do with Love*.)

As expected, my double role brought up a number of questions on the boundary between translation and production. One of these questions was around the sexuality of the Son. While the text leaves the son's sexual orientation vague, to Argentine audiences the play's hints are enough to inform an audience that the character is gay. In the Anglo world, we speak forthrightly about sexual orientation, and the play's unclarity can be read as a cue to think of the Son's orientation as complexly undefined. As a matter of translation, Ariel and I discussed whether we should retain the text's vagueness, or try to reproduce the clarity that vagueness produced for the Buenos Aires audience. A quintessential balancing act of translation: to translate the language and let its effects be foreign to us, or aim to translate the effect? In this case, we translated the language and let the anglo audience think what it might, where in other cases we made the opposite decision. In the Cherry production, the actor who played the role thought of the Son not as gay but as otherwise affectively complicated, and that acting choice worked very well.

A few of the specific dilemmas around the Son's sexual identity were quite funny: in Argentina, for a man to use artificial coffee sweetener connotes gayness as clearly and stereotypically as a pink polo shirt might in the US. Ariel and I briefly cast about for an equivalent rainbow flag, but the possibilities all forced us too far from the textual trail, and we landed on "Sweet 'n' Low," which does somehow sound queer. In production, the moment didn't produce a reliable laugh in English the way it does in Argentina, but it worked in a different way—one could tell something awkward was going on between the father and son without quite knowing what, an effect the play deploys often.

But queer flags were far from the main translation challenge before us. The play's title presents a case study in the challenges of translation. "*Pudor en animales de invierno*" literally means "The *Pudor* of Winter Animals," and

English has no equivalent for *pudor*. (The word's vestigial tail is visible in *impudence*, but none of us has "pudence.")

Ariel vetoed the standard approximations I proposed—shame, modesty, decency—all of which have their own Spanish equivalents (vergüenza, modestia, decencia). Trying to communicate the subtleties of the term to me, he noted that *pudor* is what Adam and Eve receive in the garden after they eat the apple. (Not usefully the King James Bible says "shame.") So "pudor" is the feeling we acquire at some point in childhood that nakedness (and by extension sex and other body function) is private. It touches on "modesty," "decency," and "shame," without quite being any of them.

In the body of the play, it was easy to render the word by rephrasing. *Puede que no sea frío, sino pudor.* Literally: "Maybe it wasn't cold, but *pudor.*" Speakably: "Maybe they weren't cold, maybe they didn't like being seen naked." The title was a different question. Rephrasing didn't work ("The Way Winter Animals Are Embarrassed to Be Seen Bare-Assed"?) We thought about reversing the idea ("The Nakedness of Winter Animals") but in the end decided that in English short titles are generally preferred and cut *pudor* altogether.

It's regrettable to have to drop a major theme of a play from the title, and the *pudor* of *Winter Animals* does weave deeply through the ways the Son and Father relate to their sexualities, and for that matter to their bodilyness in general. Far more than that, of course, the play requires a third actor to be the master of her own *pudor*. (The Cherry Arts' production did not use a physical refrigerator, so the naked Woman was visible, in shadow, for the entire play.)

Like the Son's sexuality, the nude Woman produces a different theatrical effect in our prudish culture than it does in the original. While I believe the majority of our upstate New York audience was able to simply accept the strange potency her naked presence added to the world of the play, some members were made uncomfortable (not necessarily a bad thing in my opinion, but anglophone audiences are not very used to being made uncomfortable). Others more thoughtfully argued that on a political level, female nudity is overused as a symbol in art, especially in contrast to male nudity. I'm sympathetic to this argument, but I would hate to cut the female nudity on its behalf. Rather, given the justification provided by the text in particular around the AIDS monologue, I could imagine a future production in which some balance was provided by the Son also spending some time in a state of impudence.

I WAS BORN TO SEE YOU SMILE

The characters are a mother and the son. Her name is Miriam. The space is neutral. The son's back is to us. He's playing with dominoes, making rows, losing himself in the game. After they fall he doesn't do anything, he stays still. She circles him, engages, approaches, moves away. As if the son were a sun and she its orbiting planet. Every so often she sits, but an impulse launches her and she rises, circles.

MIRIAM. I woke up early this morning.

Some days I wake up early. Today for example.

Early, and full of anxiety.

My heart was beating hard . . . Like this . . . pounding in my chest. I pressed. I thought it would pound its way out . . . a heart outside . . . like when your father had open-heart surgery, like that but without a scalpel, a heart put outside from sheer anxiety.

Yesterday before I went to bed I prepared everything. Actually, I'd asked dear Laura to prepare everything, but she forgot. Dear Laura has a boyfriend. Every time she gets a boyfriend, she forgets it all. Loses herself. She can't see what's important. I told her, you must make everything clean. And when I say everything I mean everything. Several shirts ironed, trousers impeccable, shoes polished, at least one change of underwear per day for a week. Or else they'll say, that one was raised in the gutter. And when I walked into your room this morning, she'd gotten out the bag and opened it, but put nothing in, just left it there. That's what happens when she gets a boyfriend. She bolts as soon as her day is done, to jump into bed with that driver I'm sure, the one that's been after her for months. At

FIGURE 3.1 (PREVIOUS PAGE) Isabel Ordaz and Nacho Sánchez in the spectacular 2017 production at the Teatro do la Abadía in Madrid, directed by Pablo Messiez. The production returned in 2018 with Fernando Delgado-Hierro in the role of the Son. *Photograph courtesy Teatro de la Abadía © Sergio Parra.*

first she didn't even like him but now you can't pry them apart. I asked her not to kiss him in the doorway, that's not the image one wants to present of this home. Let them go somewhere else to kiss. In the office, in the car, but here in my precious garden, nobody gets kissed. That little piece even told me there was a cot set up in the office of the car service. She'll sleep there, waiting for him to finish his night shift. And they just stay there, weltering like animals on that cot . . . disgusting . . . the poor creature doesn't even have the means to take her to a hotel . . .

In any case, this morning I woke up full of anxiety. I packed your bag, which little Laura hadn't packed. I put in everything. I even slipped in some chocolates. In case you get hungry at night . . . or in case it gets cold or something . . . a chocolate's always nice . . . or if you're feeling sad . . . chocolate's good for that too . . . I don't know . . . I tucked in some chocolates . . . And then . . . when I closed the clasp, I was paralyzed.

It wasn't a physical pain. It was something else. Like I'd turned to plaster.

And a thought struck me, like lightning.

I thought: I have a son who went insane . . . and this evening we're going to commit him. The sentence came to me and I murmured it out loud, like when you're not used to an idea and you have to repeat it to believe . . . "I have a son who went insane."

You know, in that moment I realized why I woke up so anxious. At night, while I slept, images of the past had come to me. In dreams, when I sleep I'm always the same age, always. I don't grow up. No more than twelve or thirteen . . . just a girl . . . I'm playing with a stick in the ground . . . I draw a line and think, this will be my life . . . I'll get married . . . I'll have a big house with lots of windows and light everywhere, and lots of children . . . and we'll all be together, holding hands, always smiling . . . and then I wake up . . . and I remember that time has passed . . . that I kept growing . . . the body grows but in dreams things stay right there, in the same place . . . a place where the future was a kind of game . . . and every so often, when I'm asleep I go back to that moment. And it's a little

FIGURE 3.2 Sánchez and Ordaz in Messiez' Abadía production, Madrid, 2017. *Photograph courtesy Teatro de la Abadía © Sergio Parra.*

frightening . . . I mean to say, I am frightened . . . this morning I woke up frightened. Nothing uglier than to start the day full of fear.

I woke up and your father had gone to work. The sun was shining through the window. I woke up crying out, and looked all around. My throat was dry, I drank some water. I always leave a glass of water beside the bed. Mama taught me that. Sometimes in the night you can get thirsty, best to have water handy. She also said that water purified dreams. Prevented nightmares. That the water would sit there all night witnessing, and at dawn you had to not drink it. The water at the side of the bed would be full of bubbles. And those are the nightmares the water held off. A nightmare for every bubble.

FIGURE 3.3 Sánchez and Ordaz in Messiez' Abadía production, Madrid, 2017. *Photograph courtesy Teatro de la Abadía © Sergio Parra.*

I never believed that stuff. I was always more rational. Anyway I drank the water. It was full of bubbles. And then I got up and went to the bathroom. On the way I stopped by your room. I looked at you while you slept. Before (I mean a long time ago) watching you sleep was so moving to me. It must be because it was always difficult for you. As a baby it took you a long time. That's why it moved me, because when I saw you asleep it was as though you'd won a battle. It was the sleep of a warrior. Sleep was always easy for me. I could lie down and fall asleep just like that. But it was always hard for you to tame your thoughts. They fight you. At any rate, I watched you sleep from the doorway. I thought, asleep like this, he seems normal.

When people sleep, they become the same. I don't know how to put it. There's something animal about sleep. Like we're all puppies when we sleep. Even old people. Sleeping shrinks us down.

You always liked it when I told you the story of Grandma. My mama's mama. On her one hundredth birthday, we had lunch at the country house, at a big table with Grandma at the head. Since I was the youngest grandchild, I was at the far other end. I watched her from there, far away, she laughed a lot, with difficulty but a lot. She toasted, she ate and drank, she didn't talk much, it was a beautiful day. We sang Happy Birthday, she blew out a hundred candles. She gave every one of us a kiss. Then she said she'd like to take a little nap. I went with her to her bed. I helped her lie down. I covered her with a quilt. I closed the door and turned out the light.

And she never woke up.

My goodness! It's true. Just look at the kind of things you liked me to tell you.

I'm going to be long-lived.

Die in my sleep, like that. In the middle of a light summer nap.

I thought all that while I looked at you. He's at peace, I thought. The demons have left him for a moment. Left him alone. Exhausted.

But back to the moment I woke up. I'm sorry to harp on it. The thing is if you can understand that moment. If you understand the color of the first moment of the day, you're likely to understand the rest.

The bed was in a mess.

The sheets were tangled. Torn.

This has been happening for a while. I don't know if it's your father or me, but one of us tears the sheets while we sleep. I change them so dear Laura won't see them when she makes up the room, so she doesn't imagine things and go out telling tales.

We spend a lot on sheets. At least once a week, I wake up with the sheets torn to ribbons.

I cut your father's nails so they stay short. I decided to cut mine too, I don't paint them or grow them long. But the sheets keep getting torn. I wake up with destruction all around.

I wake up in the remnants of a war. I get up after he does, and the first thing I do is check to see if the sheets are torn.

This morning they were. Appalling.

When I got back from your room, I went to the bathroom. I showered. I found a nylon bag and threw the sheets inside. I looked at the mattress.

FIGURE 3.4 Luz Palazon and Martin Shanly directed by Lisandro Rodriguez in the play's 2011 world premiere at Rodriguez' Elefante Club de Teatro in Buenos Aires. *Photograph by Lisandro Rodriguez.*

I always thought mattresses without sheets were rather indecent. As if there were something obscene there . . . it could belong to a nun, no matter, if I see a mattress naked it embarrasses me. As if it held dark, black secrets. That must be why I stayed and stared. The mattress had two blots down its length, it took me a minute to recognize that they were the marks of our bodies. Your father's body, and mine. That fabric with its pattern of flowers . . .

Shadows stuck to the mattress, to the fabric, over all the flowers. Your father's shadow was bigger and mine was thinner, but stronger, darker. Like the mark had been made with more force. Like my fall into the mattress was deeper. There they were, two dark bruises . . .

People in Asia don't use mattresses, they sleep on mats. They're in harmony in the Far East, night and day mix together, sleep and wakefulness aren't separate things. That's why sleep shouldn't be a division, but a passage to the next day . . . that's why they don't use mattresses, so they don't dawdle there . . . I couldn't, I couldn't sleep on a mat, no matter how transcendental it might be . . . I couldn't . . .

I threw out the sheets and went back to your room. These days I think a lot about whether you're asleep. Starting tomorrow, other people will care for your sleep. I'll have to get used to that.

When I looked I thought: well, keep sleeping, it shows you're calm. It gave me hope. A new way of hoping. That soon, one day, you'll be chatting away, just like that, like anybody . . .

Hope.

Last night, before I slept, I turned on the television. To think about something else. They were showing footage of the war. It was comforting to see lives more miserable than one's own. A woman wearing a headscarf said after the bombing, in the rubble, you could see survivors searching for their dead.

She said that after the explosion there was silence, a complete silence, a kind of brilliance. And the survivors wandered, some aimlessly; the woman said that at that moment, hope was extinguished.

And a being can't survive very long without hope, a matter of seconds, minutes at most . . . She said that during that time of wandering, she saw many people beat their heads against walls, trying clumsy ways to kill themselves.

It was the end of hope.

It's strange, but it calmed me to see that.

I told myself, I have a son who will come back, he left, but he will come back. And I have a husband sleeping beside me. I still have time.

Sometimes you find solace in other peoples' horrors.

But I'm off topic. I want to get to the point. I don't know what the point is but I want to see if I can get to it. So we can understand something, d'you know?

Alright. This morning. After I packed your bag, I took a shower.

I always liked bathing. Getting wet, being under the water. I could spend hours underwater. Mama would tell me, get out of the bathroom, you're going to wash yourself out.

They'd shut off the heater on me. It used to be different. We had a tank, not natural gas like now. Showers had to be shorter. And I needed time.

Since I was a child I felt filthy.

I always scrubbed myself a lot. Sometimes I pushed the soap so hard over my body that I left myself all red, sore.

This morning, after I packed your bag, that happened. I wanted to get that all out of my body. What was left in me of the preparations for your journey. As if I wanted the water to flood away this tangle of thoughts. To clear me.

Water cleans bodies. Bodies contain rust. Something that stains. That's what stained the mattress. The friction of bodies. Exhaustion.

I've always felt a bit of disgust. Since forever. In the shower I thought about all the things that come out of a body. The waste, the heat it radiates. All the leavings of a body. And water . . . sometimes I wish I didn't have a body, I swear I don't want one. That's the kind of thing you think about. That's why you're the way you are. You have to think about those things just every so often, not all the time or you couldn't take it.

Sometimes I'm surprised I have a body. And that you came out of it. Just like it surprises me to see branches of trees emerging from the trunk. That exact feeling, sometimes I think we're all like trees, bodies sprouting from other bodies, intertwined, budding out, more bodies . . . that's the kind of thought that came into my head there under the shower.

Then I shut off the tap. I felt cold right away. I dried myself with a clean towel.

FIGURE 3.4 Tamara Honigman and Alejandro Guerscovich directed by Gastón Díaz in a production by Grupo Salida de Emergencia at the Teatro Liebre de Marzo. This production reduced the onstage elements to two chairs and a suitcase, in front of a patterned gray wall and under a glowing white ceiling. Gualeguay, Argentina, 2015. *Photograph by Agustín Colli.*

If there's a pleasure I have in life, it's to dry off with a clean towel. It's comforting. It brings me back to myself.

When I used to bathe you before you went to school. In the beginning, when you'd let me wash you. You liked being dried the most. When I'd rub your head with the towel. I'd rub you nice and hard and you'd laugh. You'd laugh and I'd laugh. We were always laughing together. Sometimes we laugh for no reason. It drives your father crazy. We look at each other and laugh. Laughing just to laugh. We have the same laugh. We think the same things are funny. Things you can't explain. Like drying your hair. I don't know why but it always made us laugh so much.

It's been a long time since we laughed. I didn't notice when we stopped laughing. The water was falling on me and I thought, it's been a long time since anything made me laugh.

You don't laugh now.

I don't laugh.

Look at me.

Please look up.

Look at me.

I'm right here.

I'm your mama.

Your father will be here in less than an hour.

We'll put on our coats. He'll start the car. We'll bundle you in. And we'll go to the hospital.

We'll drive in silence. Night. I'll watch you in the rearview mirror. You'll be looking outside, every so often the lights will light you up. You'll be far away. We'll get to the hospital. I won't have the strength to get out. So your father will. He'll balance your bag on one shoulder as he takes you to the Reception. You'll let yourself be guided. Docile. Your violence has faded now. You'll be able to understand, a little. Like an animal that finds the hunt is already over and surrenders to the hunter. You'll let yourself be caught. No resistance.

FIGURE 3.5 Guerscovich and Honigman in the Díaz production, Gualeguay, Argentina, 2015. *Photograph by Agustín Colli.*

Going insane is losing your perimeter. Your shape. That's why your father's taking you to a place where they'll impose order. Look at me. I need you to look at me. Are you ready?

Does anything in your eyes still see me, or are you gone?

Are you still you?

I'm still me. I'm still here, inside of myself.

This day is so long. I can't encompass it all. Soon your father will get back from work and we'll have to leave and I still won't have understood what all I've lived through. This day has become eternal. The days are so long and life has become so short. It's a problem of scale.

In horror movies, there's a scene where a girl runs down a hallway fleeing peril, and the hallway gets longer and longer and she never reaches

FIGURE 3.6 Honigman and Guerscovich in the Díaz production, Gualeguay, Argentina, 2015. *Photograph by Agustín Colli.*

the end . . . that happens to me with days, they prolong, they become infinite . . . how are we going to make it to the night? . . . when your father and I get back from the hospital. When we'll eat in silence and lie down in bed.

Silence.

Look at me.

If you'd look at me for a second, I'd know what to do with you. Please look at me.

After my shower, I ate my breakfast.

When I wake up. All that time before breakfast. From the moment I wake up to the first drink of coffee. That first part of the morning, I'm uninhabited. I don't have my what-do-you-call-it. Breakfast reconstructs me.

Feed myself. Toast with cream cheese. Strong coffee with milk. In silence. Sometimes I glance at a newspaper. That's how I slowly return to being what you'd call a person. Breakfast situates me in this present. Nourish the body. Give it something material to live on.

I don't understand how hungry people survive a single day. How they stand up and make it to the night. I couldn't take being hungry. I can take anything, but not hunger. Sometimes I eat extra for fear that I'll get hungry later. I know there are people who are always hungry. I can't put myself in their place. I can't abide hunger.

I had breakfast alone because your father had gone to work. While I was having breakfast, dear Laura got here.

Where've you been?

Said I, pretending we were "besties."

I had a long night, ma'am. She answered.

I can imagine, I remarked, to keep her talking.

I don't like to talk while I breakfast. I like to listen to other people. Some days I turn on the radio and listen to those voices, I don't pay attention but they're there. Today I didn't feel like—didn't have the will to turn on the radio. So when dear Laura arrived, it was my opportunity to hear something human. Up to that moment, as I said, I was uninhabited. No words, all blank.

Did you go out with the driver?

Manuel, Señora, his name is Manuel.

You have told me that, but you know how bad I am with names.

Yes ma'am, but Manuel is an easy name.

Easy names are the hardest for me, I said, and then I scolded her for not having packed the bag.

She apologized, saying she'd had to go to the driver for an emergency. One of the sons of this Manuel had gotten into an accident in the street.

They had to look all night for a hospital and I don't know what all else. The point is, you didn't pack the bag, I said. I was about to say some more. That it's not my fault those people have children like rabbits. I only had you. And I have to take care of you. That's what I said: Laura, I trust you to take care of my son, I'm not interested in what happened to Manuel's son. Señora, it was serious, she insisted. I'm not even interested in hearing your story, Laura. My toast stuck in my throat when I said that. I started coughing, she gave me a slap on the back, I motioned her away.

I don't know why. I'd wanted to just listen, but I interrupted her. Well, at that moment I realized I wanted even more to vent something, to rid myself of an anger that had overtaken me when I became conscious of the day, I wanted to explode more than I wanted to sit quietly listening.

Calm down, ma'am, she told me. I will not calm down Laura. You know what we're going through and you go to the driver with everything half-finished. I'm sure you went to wallow in that disgusting cot, while I'm here with this son who is not well. You don't care about anything Laura, you don't care. There's something called loyalty. A thing you don't have. Ma'am, but Manuel's son was almost killed. Don't you keep going Laura, do not keep going. Let me finish my breakfast in peace. Look what you've done to me. You've made me angry. Please leave, Laura. Let it pass. As you wish, ma'am, she said, impertinently.

She left and I was furious. I had a drink of coffee. I got to the end of the cup. Fury had made me alert. Yes indeed, I was awake now. Now I had to calm down. I breathed deeply. I moved my head, my neck creaked. I looked out the window. A cloudy day.

You like cloudy days. They're hard on me.

That even light over everything. It's hard on me. I knew this day was going to be hard on me.

Then I felt the cold. I could just say, I got cold. But actually I'd been cold since I woke up.

FIGURE 3.7 Sánchez and Ordaz in Messiez' Abadía production, Madrid, 2017. *Photograph courtesy Teatro de la Abadía © Sergio Parra.*

After breakfast. When Laura left the kitchen. I became aware of the cold. I realized that my body was contracted with the cold. That I'd been cold all night. Breakfast had reanimated the cold.

And just like I can't take being hungry, I can't stand being cold. Especially not when it's an unmanageable cold, when you don't know where it comes from. And you begin to suspect it's an internal cold. A cold that comes from within, from the entrails. A cold that fixes itself in the body and leaves you with nothing. That's the sort of cold I felt.

A shiver ran through me.

I hate the shivers. Losing control of the stillness of my body. I called Laura. She walked in without looking at me. Are you cold? I asked. No ma'am, it's not cold. It's not cold at all here.

Then I thought of you. We'd have to pack more coats for you. You might be cold, in the institution. We're alike that way. That way as well. We're both cold-blooded.

The chemicals will make the cold go away. I saw other sick people in the hospital courtyard, half-naked in the middle of winter.

Or maybe insanity produces heat. Suffocation. The fire that burns them from within.

Look at me.

Are you cold?

Do you want me to hug you?

Where are you right now? Far? Near?

Bipolar. The two poles. You should be cold like the arctic. But no, you're hot. So much heat in your body.

Or it's something else. Forgetting of the body. Of the body temperature.

The sick people in the yard of the institution didn't feel hot. What they felt was the refusal to feel. No feeling, not even cold.

Being warm or cold is a fact. It belongs to the body. But at the same time, it's a state of consciousness.

In the morning. When I felt myself shiver, I stood up and turned on the hot water in the sink. Let it run. I put my hands under the stream. My blood began warming inward from the fingertips to my chest. It turned my soul around. I kept my hands under the water. That warmth arriving.

The same as the cold. There are days when the heat takes me off guard. I'm suddenly out of air. I open all the windows. I drink cold water but it doesn't go away.

I'm a broken appliance. I can't regulate my temperature. I need a moderate climate. Temperate. Neutral.

This body is changing. This. My life.

I need you to understand what I was thinking about, with my hands in that stream of water.

I thought. I have a life.

I thought about Laura, angry in the other room.

About the driver.

About your father.

And I thought about you. You don't know how often I think of you these days.

I thought, there are all these lives. All of your lives. When I walk down the street, I look at people and all that life surprises me. All those lives that aren't mine.

I thought: dear Laura has a life, I don't know what kind of life it will be but in whatever case, it's a life. You have a life. Or you're going to have one, if you get out of this. Your father has a life. All these lives together and the only one you can know is your own. The other lives—the lives of others—you can only know the surface.

My life, my hands under the jet of hot water. My life, this heat, this is reality.

And I am in reality.

A person can be in reality, or not.

I chose to stay. You left.

When I look at all those unknown people. I think each one of them has a reality. Something palpable. Us. You and me. We are material. I can approach and touch you. That is reality. This materiality. To accept that my hand is warm and losing its cold. Blood rushing and pounding. The pain of muscles. Saliva, sweat. That is reality. I am in reality. I am reality. Not you. You left. You left me here, alone. I am alone in reality.

In reality, I am alone.

Oof, I scared myself.

I just got scared.

I took advantage of the flowing water to wash the cup. I justified the water's flow. I realized I'd only turned on the faucet to wash the cup. I went back and sat at the table. I doodled with my fingertip in the crumbs the

FIGURES 3.7–8 Sánchez and Ordaz in Messiez' Abadía production, Madrid, 2017. *Photographs courtesy Teatro de la Abadía © Sergio Parra.*

toast had left behind. The day was just beginning. It will be a long day. I murmured. What was that, ma'am? Laura asked from the living room. Nothing, I didn't say anything.

We're going to have a long day.

In less than an hour, your father will be here.

Two hours later, you'll be in a room at the clinic.

I packed a sweater in case you get cold. I'm sure the place is heated. But sometimes, at dawn, if you wake up, if you feel like going out in the backyard. At any rate, I packed a sweater just in case.

FIGURE 3.9 Sánchez in Messiez' Abadía production, Madrid, 2017. *Photograph courtesy Teatro de la Abadía © Sergio Parra.*

Then I left the kitchen and went to your room. To wake you up. To give you your medicine. To try to give you a bath.

There was a lot of light. And you were curled up. You were smiling.

When I was a girl, I was lazy.

It was hard for me to get up in the morning. I hated that light. The cruel morning light that illuminates too much and leaves no shadows. The day violently advancing on the earth. The flat light of the morning.

As a girl, I'd steal Mama's dark glasses. I'd wear them to go out on the street. To filter the light. Mama took them back. She said dark glasses were for grown-up women. That girls couldn't wear them. She took them from me. But as soon as she stopped paying attention I'd put them on again.

FIGURE 3.10 Ordaz and Sánchez in Messiez' Abadía production, Madrid, 2017. *Photograph courtesy Teatro de la Abadía © Sergio Parra.*

She slapped me once, she said: at your age, only whores and blind people wear dark glasses.

I didn't try it again. I'm not blind nor a whore. I spent my childhood with eyes irritated by decorum. It was years before I wore sunglasses again. That must have been around the time I wore a miniskirt. Don't laugh, your mother once wore tiny miniskirts, very short.

Miniskirts and sunglasses.

In time, I've started to avoid going out when the sun is intense. I stay at home, in this dim light. I prefer the gloom to that hard midday sun.

When I have to go out for some reason, sunglasses or no, I'm dazzled. That inordinate light. It's a bad dream. I walk down the street, on the asphalt, and I'm overlit. The midday light. Like being awake, but too much.

I've never been more awake than today.

And that has nothing to do with light. It's something else. When the day started, I didn't know I was going to feel this awake, too awake.

I approached your face. I leaned over you and kissed you on the forehead. You let out a tiny moan. Another time I would have missed that moan, but today I heard it, and it upset me. It was an animal moan. A moan from your body. Like a reflex.

In your sleep you were protected. I pulled you out of a place of shelter. I can understand that.

The thing is, your father and I have made the decision. We're going to commit you.

FIGURE 3.11 Honigman and Guerscovich in the Díaz production, Gualeguay, Argentina, 2015. *Photograph by Agustín Colli.*

One day you'll understand. Not today.

We have no more to give.

I stroked your whole body. I dropped to your side. The bed was damp. I sat up, disgusted. I thought, you've wet the bed. You'd do that as a child.

Every time I scolded you, that same night. You'd wet the bed. And I had to change the sheets. Or I'd put a towel around you to not wake you up.

It was hard for me to scold you. It tore my soul. I never hit you. How can a person strike a child? I never understood things like that.

So you had wet the bed. You were back to being a scared child. Your nocturnal revenge. I stripped the sheets. The hot water bottle had leaked. Who put in this hot water bottle? I did, ma'am, says Laura, the little guy was shivering so I put in a hot water bottle.

FIGURE 3.12 Guerscovich and Honigman in the Díaz production, Gualeguay, Argentina, 2015. *Photograph by Agustín Colli.*

He was shivering from his ravings, Laura, not from cold. And if you put that bottle in, you should have checked it was sealed. What if it scalded him during the night.

He didn't wake up, ma'am, he didn't wake up. All wet and he didn't wake up. He slept in that swamp of wet sheets, my poor sweet boy.

He still isn't awake, help me Laura, we'll take him to the bathroom. We tried to lift you up between the two of us. But it was impossible. Sometimes I forget you have a big body.

I would hold you all day. If it were up to me, you'd never have left my arms. He's a year old, it's time to see if he can walk on his own. No, he's still small. My back hurt but I wouldn't put you down for anything. All day with

FIGURE 3.13 Sánchez in Messiez' Abadía production, Madrid, 2017. *Photo-graph courtesy Teatro de la Abadía © Sergio Parra.*

me. Stuck together. My appendix. When I put you down, you'd cry. It took you a long time to get used to your body being just you. Without me.

It took me much longer.

Your father was jealous. The love we had didn't compare to yours and mine.

The love story between your father and I is very short. We met on that yacht, introduced by a mutual friend. Six months of dating. The wedding. The pregnancy. The rest is boring. Nothing to tell.

By contrast, the love story with a son is complex. A son comes out of you. It's a detachment from the body. Something that took form there, and emerges. And you look at that thing in amazement.

FIGURE 3.14 Sánchez and Ordaz in Messiez' Abadía production, Madrid, 2017. *Photograph courtesy Teatro de la Abadía © Sergio Parra.*

What I mean is, I've held you so deep inside, I know you better than I ever came to know myself.

Wouldn't you say?

Look at me.

Since we couldn't lift you in our arms, Laurita and I dragged you to the bathroom. It was hard for me. Not for her. She has the brute force of the people who do that kind of work . . . service work I mean . . . I couldn't serve other people, I don't have the physique for it, not the patience either. I was born to be served. I'm good at giving orders. It's not as easy as you think to give an order. Don't contradict yourself, don't hesitate. Don't confuse the help. It's something you learn over time. I learned to command. At least some things . . .

We turn on the shower and push you down in the tub to wake you up. Laura got wet, you opened your eyes and panicked. Laura laughed her head off, I'm at the water park, señora! She was all wet. You looked at her. You looked at her, not at me. The bathroom was a disaster. Water everywhere. Everything was wet. Your bed. The bathroom, all this wetness and the cold.

Laura and I take your clothes off. I should warn you, dear Laura is quite familiar with your body.

We leave you naked. You look at us, naked from the bathtub.

Before your father, I'd never seen a man naked. Once at school, on a poster. But not in reality. The day I saw your father, it gave me a little giggle. He noticed and was embarrassed. Your father had more experience with that sort of thing.

Then I saw you naked. Since you were born. The day you were born, we were both naked. In that moment, all the things that are usually covered are exposed.

Then I saw you grow up. I bathed you. Until one day, suddenly, you were embarrassed I could see you. I was angry at first, then I understood. Now you needed privacy. Your father explained that.

Your father explained a lot of things to me. Your father cultivated me. I wasn't like that before. I improved with time. I wasn't refined, not cultured, or observant. I learned all that.

I also had time to do it, but others don't. I read. A book your father brought me was a book I read. That got me in the habit. One's alone time. Then I'd go to the bookstore and ask about the month's new books. Nothing complicated, something you can read without yawning. I read everything. I learned to be curious, too. To have a topic of conversation. If you don't read, what is there to talk about. When you go out with your husband, to a work meeting for example, the husband expects you to have topics of conversation. That's what reading is for, to have things to talk about, otherwise why read at all? Concentrating, turning the pages, getting to the end, it's all quite a chore.

But I never read those books you did. I borrowed some from you but I couldn't understand them. They were crude books. Boring. I don't know how you got into reading that kind of thing. Not all reading is healthy. I should have taken away those books before it was too late. You read too much. You didn't go out. Sometimes you wouldn't even get up to turn on the light when night was falling. You'd be still, reading. Then I'd walk by your door and turn on the light. And you'd look up at me with that empty look. And I'd lower my eyes. I'd move away. I knew you were gone during all those hours.

In the bathroom, you looked at Laura and me with that same look. Someone else in your place. Naked in front of two women you should be embarrassed. Try to cover up. You there like it was nothing.

That's what insanity is. The loss of modesty. That's why insanity is dirty. It's obscene.

Look at me.

There's so little time before your father comes and we go to the hospital.

I don't want to commit you.

I have no choice.

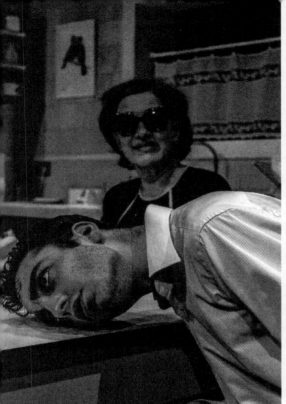

FIGURES 3.15–16 Sánchez and Ordaz in Messiez' Abadía production, Madrid, 2017. *Photographs courtesy Teatro de la Abadía © Sergio Parra.*

No options.

Option 1: Home hospitalization.

Option 2: Clinical hospitalization.

Option 3: Escape.

You're the same age your father was when I saw him naked.

Your body is nothing like his.

He was rougher. Massive. You have a delicate body. Soft.

I can look at your nakedness like it's not a man's. A kind of total nudity. Naked even of sex. A nakedness without identity.

We have to get the smell out, Laura. All sick people smell bad. Then we have to open the windows of his room. Even if it gets cold. Even if it's hard for us. Open all the windows, make that smell of sickness go away. Let the healthy air come back in.

Don't look at me like that.

Please don't look at me.

My throat hurts.

I yelled. I hurt my throat.

I used to take care of my throat. In time, I stopped caring. My voice got coarse. At one point, I wanted to sing in the church choir.

I must have been fifteen. No older.

When I heard the chorus at Mass, my eyes filled with tears. I levitated. All those voices in glorious intersection. Those angelic praises. I wanted to lose my voice among all those voices. To unite with them, fuse my voice in that collective song.

One day, they gave me a test. The music teacher who directed the chorus closed the door. She settled her pleated skirt and sat elegantly, ready to listen to me.

Everything became silent.

I sang the songs that I'd sung alone, in secret.

I saw the teacher's face shift. She lost her serenity and twitched. A twist of disgust in her mouth. As if she'd bitten into a rotten fruit and was about to throw up.

I had a dreadful voice. I didn't know until that day. Up to that moment, I had always whisper-sung, softly.

Sometimes one doesn't know the truth until others name it. That happened to me with my voice.

She asked me to stop, to not continue. She raised her hands to her ears. I turned red. I wanted to run.

It's alright, she said. It's only your voice, you may have a talent for something else.

Can my voice can be fixed, I asked.

Your voice is irrecuperable. Ugly.

I was about to cry and she stopped me. She proposed that I sing in the choir but without a voice. Just mouth without making sounds.

I said yes. I wanted to be part of the choir.

And there I was, moving my lips on Sundays. Borrowing a voice. I learned to sing in silence. To sing on the inside.

Look at me.

Say something to me.

Now you know more about your mother than I've known about you in this whole life.

Look at me.

Where have you gone?

It's made me sad to talk about all this.

I can't go on.

Laura, you finish washing him. Scrub him well. Get off all the grime.

Laura gives you head massages.

Your head would hurt.

My head hurt me all my life.

Permanent migraines.

You can't tell the difference. I thought, he has a headache. Like his mother. Mother and son both suffer from migraines, nothing more than that. But no.

After the pain came insanity. The pain was a sign. It was part of the coming undone. Rub him, Laura, rub well. Massage his head and calm his thoughts.

Your father will be here so soon and we're still not ready.

FIGURE 3.17 Honigman and Guerscovich in the Díaz production, Gualeguay, Argentina, 2015. *Photograph by Agustín Colli.*

FIGURE 3.18 Honigman and Guerscovich in the Díaz production, Gualeguay, Argentina, 2015. *Photograph by Agustín Colli.*

She changed you. She put on your best clothes. And I turned away, I didn't want to look at you. My throat knotted.

I've been thinking it since that moment.

I think. This boy followed me.

My son.

Look at me. I'm going to explain it to you. A person contains something. I mean has something inside.

In the depths.

In an inner cavern. Remote.

At the root, this is not who I am.

I am fire and blood. Fury.

FIGURE 3.19 Ordaz in Messiez' Abadía production, Madrid, 2017. *Photograph courtesy Teatro de la Abadía © Sergio Parra.*

I am something else, something I don't know.

You came from deep in there.

That's why you became flesh.

You are my continuation. That's why I know you so well. Better than you'll ever be able to understand.

I am at your beginning and I'll be at your end.

We don't have long, just a few minutes.

We still have time.

We can run.

If you want, we'll go away together.

Before your father comes.

You won't be committed.

I know where he keeps the money.

I'll get my things together and we'll go.

Together.

You and me.

I could devour you.

Make you mine.

Even more mine.

We'll tell Laura to lock the door. Say nothing.

We'll give her some of what we steal. She can come visit later.

We'll go.

We'll take a plane.

To Brazil. We'll buy a house.

We'll make an inn at the side of the ocean.

You'll spend your days in the water.

Water heals.

We'll change our names.

We'll have a simple life.

By the sea.

We'll live in a house without light. Far from everyone.

Every so often, travelers will come. Strangers will stay for a couple of days and leave. People who have no history with us.

And you and I will grow old.

We'll be alone.

Far away.

In that quiet house.

You can only hear the sea. Nothing else. Forever.

And one day you'll die. In my arms.

I'll bury you in the sand. Deep down.

I'll wait for years to pass before I go.

I'll get even older.

Evenings I'll walk on the beach.

Barefoot. With difficulty.

Serene.

Look at me.

Do you want us to leave?

You have to look at me.

No?

We'll stay.

We'll commit you and you'll get better?

They'll take care of you there.

You like to be protected.

I got sad.

Look at me.

I'm calm.

You're going to be okay.

Look at me.

You smiled!

You smiled. I am illuminated.

I was born for that.

Just for that.

I was born to see you smile.

Other people have other missions in life. That one is mine. Your smile.

Let me embrace you.

Before your father comes and we put you in the car.

I'm going to hold you.

I want to fold you close.

This moment.

THE END

FIGURE 3.20 The "ghost bedroom" in Rodriguez' Elefante Club premiere. Buenos Aires, 2011. *Photograph by Lisandro Rodriguez.*

TRANSLATOR/EDITOR'S NOTE

My relationship to *I Was Born to See You Smile* feels distinct from the others in this book, because it is the only play that, at the time of this writing, I've not seen produced in either Spanish or English. I am delighted that it joins us here not only for its own gorgeous qualities, but also for the resonances it reveals among other plays by Loza. On the one hand, a version of the troubled sleepless son we meet in *Winter Animals* (in part a version of young Loza) is also fretted over, here, by a concerned, helpless parent, but in this case, the son is much more tragically far gone. This parent, on the other hand, is very much not the simple-presenting but deceptively deep rural father of *Winter Animals* (who shares those qualities with the Girl in *The Saint*, the last play in this collection). Rather, she's a petty bourgeoise incapable of perceiving her own heartlessness toward the working class—a quality taken to its logical conclusion by the characters of the next play, *Altitude Sickness*. Like many of Loza's heroines, Miriam speaks her truth after a lifetime of silence imposed on her by class, but Miriam's silence has been imposed on her by privilege rather than by poverty, an interesting switch and one that makes her final *cri de coeur* no less heartrending.

Technical translation questions here were small but thought-provoking. Miriam says "mamá" and "papá" throughout the play. Since her way of talking is elegant and often poetically heightened, "Mom" and "Dad" sounded wrong. We found that when she speaks of her mother, the slightly old-fashioned "mama" felt right, but when she talks to her son about "tu papá," "your papa" sounded goofy, "dad" too informal, "your father" just right. These are micro questions, but the interest to me was that the words we chose weren't justified by the words they reference in the original, but rather by the character voice that emerged as a whole. (In a similar vein, we found that Miriam "wanted" to say "Laurita" as "dear Laura"—until, halfway into the play, she didn't.)

I Was Born to See You Smile was also the site of a tiny but memorable translation breakthrough that affected another play in this volume. Miriam twice says, "como quien dice," which looks like "as some folks say." But I'd been through this conversation with Ariel before: "as some folks say" almost never works in context (the phrase never seems to reference something folks particularly say). I asked Ariel once and for all to please explain what the heck "como quien dice" means. Not for the first time, he said, "It's truly not important, Sam. We can cut it and not lose anything." "But what does it add to the sentence?" I insisted. He was getting annoyed. "I keep telling you, it adds nothing to the meaning. It's just . . . filler words. I guess you don't have them in English." Lightbulb. Do we ever have them. Spoken English is chock-a-block with filler words—*like, so, anyway, you know?* Versions of these filler phrases made the translated English sentences sing. It was another reminder that the theater translator should think about what phrases do, rather than what they mean.

I was especially excited about this nerdy micropoint because Ariel and I had first had the conversation while working on *Nothing to Do with Love.* As it turns out, the Seamstress says "como quien dice" very often, almost becoming a verbal signature. In that translation, which was by this time two years old, I'd satisfied myself with either cutting the phrase or having her say, "as they say" about a thing that nobody says. Now, the Seamstress says, "don't you know" a lot, don't you know, and it's a lovely part of what makes her who she is.

ALTITUDE SICKNESS

1

MANU. We were walking, holding hands.

We'd just had a fight. She grabbed my hand.

Squeezed it.

As if she knew it was ending and the pressure of her hand was the final possible thing. She didn't want to let go.

I said it. Look, it's better for us to end this now instead of continuing in agony.

She lowered her head like she was agreeing. We stayed silent. I paid the bill. She wanted to put in money, I said no. Better to save it I said, when you have to move you're gonna need money. She didn't say anything, she swallowed. We got up and walked together in silence.

This really fine rain started to fall. The kind of rain that slowly penetrates your clothes and into your skin. There was almost nobody in the street. She squeezed my hand again.

And I thought, the rain, this empty avenue, the lights, the cars going by. These are the images of our breakup. The breakup itself is almost redundant. This is the breakup we deserve.

"We're in a breakup cliché. The city arranged to bid a poetic farewell to our love."

I said it as a joke, I didn't know if it would make her laugh. I thought it would leave things clear. But the warmth of her hand was strong

FIGURE 4.1 (PREVIOUS PAGE) Pablo Cura, Natalia Señorales, Patricio Aramburu, and Julián Krakov in Cristian Drut's production at the Abasto Social Club, Buenos Aires, 2013. In quintessential Buenos Aries's "off-circuit" style, Drut made a virtue of scarcity, with a shadowy, atmospheric production footlit in saturated color and pressed against a white-painted brick wall. *Photograph by Sol Pittau.*

and damp, I don't know from the rain or from sweat. She's shaking, I thought.

She's not going to survive, I said to myself. She can't without me.

I was thinking all this while we were walking through the park. Across from that monument three or four blocks off, the one of the hero on horseback—for years I thought it was General San Martín but someone told me it's not. Anyway, we were walking and suddenly I see this filthy guy, he crosses right in front of us to a lamppost, opens his zipper, pulls out his dick and starts to take a piss.

I stop, paralyzed, I'm shocked. I try to keep walking but the image is so strong. If she saw it, our final moment, this walk, will have been destroyed by this image.

I mean the whole moment, the very fine rain and the city saying farewell is gonna come second to the beggar with his dick out, leaning on the lamppost like it was a huge effort to stay standing while he unloads.

If she sees that. If that's what she remembers. We'll have had the most disgusting breakup in history.

And the relationship will be inseparable. The breakup will be tied to the hobo's dick. To that liquid sound of the piss on the post. That disgust.

What kind of a world are we living in when you can't even break up with your girlfriend to an acceptable image?

TINO. Did she see it?

MANU. I don't know. We didn't talk about it.

We got back to the apartment. I brushed my teeth. I went to bed. She stayed in the bathroom.

I closed my eyes and immediately fell asleep. When I feel guilty I fall asleep, it never fails.

But in that moment. Before sleep. That final image. Was that dude, pissing leaning against the lamppost.

FIGURE 4.2 Aramburu, Cura, Krakov, and Señorales in Drut's Abasto production, Buenos Aires, 2013. *Photograph by Sol Pittau.*

TINO. You went to sleep to the image of that hobo's dick.

MANU. Yeah, I've been wondering for days now.

TINO. What?

MANU. About whether it means something.

TINO. You think?

MANU. Totally. It's no accident. We were walking, it was the exact moment, and the dude crosses and pisses.

TINO. Maybe you made him feel like it, or, he just couldn't hold it, you know, the damp, the rain . . . I mean, as soon as I hear rain I wanna take a piss.

MANU. No, this dude could've taken a piss anytime. But the way he did it, it was planned. Like a lame movie. We were breaking up in this perfect

FIGURE 4.3 Krakov, Señorales, Cura, and Aramburu in Drut's Abasto production, Buenos Aires, 2013. *Photograph by Sol Pittau.*

way, I don't know if you get me. The rain, the lights, empty streets, cars, the night. All of a sudden interrupted by this raggedy dude's zipper.

TINO. Did he look at you?

MANU. What?

TINO. Did he look at you while he was pissing.

Then you might suspect he'd planned it.

MANU. I couldn't see if he was looking at me.

I looked away. I was praying she hadn't noticed the image.

TINO. Well, did she?

MANU. I don't know.

TINO. You didn't ask?

MANU. The next day everything was really sad, it didn't seem like the right time to bring up the hobo and his dick.

TINO. But after? You couldn't ask her?

MANU. She came to get her stuff last Friday. It crossed my mind before she went down to the taxi, to ask her about that night, but I couldn't do it. Days have gone by, they're gonna keep going by, I want to avoid leaving her with that memory.

TINO. You don't even know if she has it. C'mon, maybe she didn't see it, maybe she didn't give it any importance, maybe she forgot about it. I'm sure she was too distracted to notice.

MANU. It was a very potent image, a level of disgusting that tattoos itself on your retina. It was a disaster. I thought. Our love. All our love reduced to this. Love is a bum pissing on a lamppost under the fine night rain with cars passing, and the silence and the water in all its forms.

TINO. You're making this too important.

MANU. And the sound, I can still hear it. The liquid slapping the lamppost. A liquid that'll rust a lamppost, bit by bit eating away the metal. Abrasive, acidic. Invisible by day but secretly active, corroding. Bit by bit. Leaving its marks and stains.

TINO. You're taking this very hard.

MANU. Consciously or unconsciously, that bum left his signature. On us at least. Like initialing the bottom of a document. The end of our love, signed in a hobo's urine. That is the death of love. That's where it ends. Don't look.

TINO. It's OK, shhhhh. I don't think she saw it.
When you break up with girls, they get introspective. I don't think she saw it.

MANU. God willing.

TINO. This is a God thing?

MANU. Please God don't let her have seen it.

RAMO. Have you ever noticed that early in the morning there's nobody begging in the train.

I take the train at six. Every day. Beggars never show up then. Nobody selling anything, playing music, putting out their hands. Nothing.

TINO. I hadn't noticed.

RAMO. We're the ones that get up every morning. Every day. At the same time. They're the ones who stay in their caves, waiting, comfortable, sleeping till the day's underway.

MANU. It must be weird to ride a train without anyone asking for change.

TINO. I can't imagine it.

MANU. I never get up that early. I mean, I never take the train either.

RAMO. I'm that average dude who takes the train downtown every morning.

I even had a wife, 'til she left me.

I'm still in the habit . . . I used to say a couple words when I left the bedroom in the morning. Like a kind of key. And she'd answer, and the day would officially start, I could go out on the street. Every day.

TINO. What stuff would you say?

MANU. Last night I had a dream. I was dressed like a woman. I was in a long skirt, the hem was dragging on the floor, it was getting dirty. I pulled it up and under the skirt I was wearing a gold lamé thong, a horrible thing, I woke up screaming.

RAMO. I was watching the landscape from the train. I was moving and the scenery was staying in place. I was getting further away. During the day, there's no scenery there. Or maybe I'm just not thinking there is. I don't know. I can't see it. I'm at the computer, and every so often this thought jumps into my head, during all these hours what's going on with the scenery I saw from the train? Who's looking at that scenery?

TINO. Don't get melancholy. She's gonna come back.

It takes a while but they come back.

RAMO. Scenery is only scenery when someone's looking at it.

MANU. Don't talk crazy, this isn't the time to rethink everything.

RAMO. . . . it takes a while but they come back.

MANU. All morning I felt like I was wearing the thong. I went to the bathroom two or three times and pulled down my pants to make sure I wasn't wearing the gold lamé thong. I swear I could feel it. I thought, if I'm in an accident, if they have to take me to the hospital and cut off my pants cause they need to operate, they're gonna discover the thong. The whole idea made me sweat. I couldn't concentrate.

TINO. I just had to go to the dentist.

Why do dentists give out appointments they don't respect?

FIGURE 4.4 Cura, Señorales, Krakov, and Aramburu in Drut's Abasto production, Buenos Aires, 2013. *Photograph by Sol Pittau.*

I waited almost an hour.

What do you do while you're waiting?

I looked at the receptionist.

I thought about the kind of life she must have.

She wasn't ugly, not pretty either, some intermediate thing, a hybrid.

She was bored. She had to have noticed I was looking because she looked up.

MANU. Was she uncomfortable?

TINO. I pretended I got a text message. I started playing on the phone. I entered a number, I went back to looking at her. I wondered what

FIGURE 4.5 Cura, Señorales, Aramburu, and Krakov in Drut's Abasto production, Buenos Aires, 2013. *Photograph by Sol Pittau.*

kind of life I could have with the dental receptionist. I thought a dental receptionist probably didn't have a lot of ambition, so I thought her job was probably pretty low-stress—we'd probably have good sex at night. I thought we probably wouldn't have too much to talk about, and that would be OK. I thought we might have two kids, the older one would be named Octavio, the younger one after a lot of arguing we'd have named José for his grandfather who died the year before. I thought I'd never be able to really love the younger son because I didn't choose his name.

I thought she'd be a good mother, a bit possessive though. I thought she'd probably be a good cook and I felt a bit hungry. I thought I'd get a bite to eat after my appointment. I thought I'd have anesthesia in my mouth and it'd be hard to chew. I thought about standing up and demanding punctuality. I thought that I could seize the moment to kiss her on the lips. I thought her breath would be sweet, like caramel. I thought she had nice teeth and that was the only reason they hired her. I thought she was the dentist's lover. I thought she'd always betray me with the dentist. No matter what happened she would always end up with him. I thought about all the power of a dentist. I thought she'd be happy while every day he looked at her teeth.

RAMO. It's hot in here.

TINO. It's getting dark out.

There's a storm. Could rain pretty hard.

MANU. The sky was a weird color. Dirty yellow.

RAMO. It could be dust particles. The sun, the clouds, all sifted through this floating earth. There were swirls of it, low, close to the train. When it went by, in some places it made swirls.

MANU. Last night, before I went to sleep, I thought about her again. I thought about all the bad points.

I made a list, pros and cons. I tried to do a balance sheet.

I started to mix up the good with the bad. I started to blink, I got dizzy, I couldn't stay lying down, I got up, I went to the window. I had a cigarette and then another and another and that's how I spent the night. The sky started to get light. A brilliant yellow. I stood there watching while that yellow appeared and then the wind came up. The cigarettes were gone and I said, I'm gonna quit smoking.

Actually, I think I don't miss her. That's what scared me. You find one day you've stopped missing someone. It's frightening.

I was really thirsty. I drank water but the thirst didn't go away.

RAMO. You have something in your left eye.

MANU. Here?

RAMO. I don't see it now. It was a glint.

Might've been the light, it plays tricks sometimes.

3

PAMELA. Manu never liked my name.

That's a thing you should pay attention to. Notice those tiny details.

He called me Pam.

Who gets called Pam?

What kind of a nickname is that?

Pamela.

I confronted him one day. I asked him: What does my name make you think of?

At first he pretended not to hear me. But he was always a terrible liar.

You could tell the "name" question made him uncomfortable.

Citrus fruits, he said.

I told him not to be literal, just 'cause it's two letters off pomelo it shouldn't suggest fruitiness, tartness, juice. You just wait, I said to him. Words are destiny. You can't avoid them with abbreviation. The word is still in there, just condensed.

Fine Pam, he said, just don't make me say your whole name.

That's not gonna be easy for me, I said. If you can't say my name, this isn't gonna be easy.

Nothing's easy. He said.

Mornings, I mean waking up next to someone who won't say your name.

I mean love is also wanting to say a name. Whisper it, doodle it in notebooks, you know. I'm talking about love.

TINO. Did it just get cold in here or is it my body?

I just ate a hot dog. As soon as I eat something, my body goes cold for a bit, then it goes away.

PAMELA. What time did you say he was coming?

TINO. We usually meet up around this time.

They're late today. Might be the storm.

PAMELA. It stopped raining two hours ago, it's not an excuse.

TINO. But there are trees down, the streets are muddy.

PAMELA. When you want to show up, no storm is strong enough.

TINO. I'm not sure about that, Pamela.

I'm not that convinced that's true.

PAMELA. What's true?

TINO. About wanting to show up, and the storm.

PAMELA. I just said it to say something. I wasn't really thinking.

Just killing time. Filling the silence.

It wasn't meant to be deep reflection.

TINO. I've been feeling vulnerable lately.

PAMELA. Yeah, I can tell.

TINO. But let's not talk about me, we were talking about you guys.

PAMELA. Who?

TINO. You. Manu. Love.

PAMELA. Oh yeah, I got distracted for a sec.

TINO. Happens.

PAMELA. Sometimes it's hard to stay on the subject.

TINO. The opposite happens to me.

PAMELA. What.

TINO. Once I get on a subject, on my subject, I can't get off it, I obsess.

PAMELA. Then you were being generous, you didn't impose. You let me expand on mine.

TINO. You're a woman, I'm not a savage, I let you go on. But it doesn't mean I was paying attention.

PAMELA. You weren't listening?

TINO. A bit. Barely.

PAMELA. That's sad. I was about to say it had been a long time since somebody really listened to me like that.

TINO. Sorry.

PAMELA. It's hard to find someone good at listening.

TINO. Yeah, it's tough.

PAMELA. Anyway. You were making good faces. It looked like you were listening.

TINO. I do it at work too. Those faces. I nod. Raise my eyebrows. Move my head a little. It always works, but in reality I'm far away. It's like leaving it to the management, delegating tasks.

PAMELA. I don't understand the metaphor.

TINO. It's basically three or four moves. Maybe more when you combine them. It takes four gestures to look attentive.

PAMELA. Anyway, it was very nice of you.

TINO. Thanks.

PAMELA. I got a little cold too.

TINO. Maybe the temperature did go down.

PAMELA. The sky was really weird. The clouds were fat, like snow clouds.

TINO. It might snow. Happened once, it could happen again.

PAMELA. Did Manu tell you he hates my name?

TINO. I'm not gonna say what we talk about between ourselves.

PAMELA. One day I made him spell it out, I thought it would cure his phobia.

It was cruel but I did it. And I saw him perform it, but inside he was twisting away from every letter. Like they scratched.

TINO. It shouldn't be this cold this time of year. It's not normal.

PAMELA. I didn't come to talk about the weather, sorry but I'm in no mood for some kind of trivial conversation. At least not right now.

TINO. They might not come.

Sometimes they don't come.

PAMELA. And you hang out alone?

TINO. Sometimes I don't even come myself.

PAMELA. And what happens then?

TINO. Everything's the same, just empty.

PAMELA. It sucks, I didn't bring a coat and I'm gonna be cold.

4

RAMO. He says he misses you every now and then. Not all the time, sometimes not at all. But that's how it is, no one misses anyone all the time. Just intermittently.

PAMELA. Good thing I brought this sweater, last time I was dying of cold.

RAMO. But when he says your name, his eyes fill with tears. It's instantaneous. He says your name and he tears up. It's kind of moving.

PAMELA. Almost no sun gets in here. It can't warm it up enough. We shouldn't be this cold this time of year.

RAMO. He told me he kept the notes you left stuck to the refrigerator. He keeps them carefully, goes back and looks at them. Grocery lists, dentist-appointment reminders, plus some little sketches you did with half your brain while you were talking on the phone.

PAMELA. It makes me feel a bit better that he says my name.

I'm happy he managed that.

RAMO. Sometimes it's hard to say a name.

PAMELA. It's happened with every guy I've been with. They couldn't say my name.

RAMO. It doesn't matter. You can name a person a lot of different ways.

PAMELA. It made me feel anonymous.

RAMO. There were a couple of street kids outside, couldn't have been more than twelve years old, yelling, going through the garbage. I can't handle it anymore, it's disgusting.

PAMELA. Did he ask if I was seeing anybody?

RAMO. . . . now that I think about it, no, he never asked me that.

He asked some stuff, but not that . . . weird.

PAMELA. Maybe he's not interested.

RAMO. I walked up to the two kids and said to them, don't you guys have a mother, doing that? . . . doing what?, they asked. Going through the garbage, leaving all this crap all over the grass.

PAMELA. You didn't have to ask them anything.

It wasn't your business.

RAMO. I have the right to look at clean grass. I have that right as a citizen. To hygiene, to not smell bad smells, to a spotless landscape.

PAMELA. I don't think I miss him, but there are things I'm not sure about.

The last few times a weird thing happened.

RAMO. What's that?

PAMELA. When we were talking.

We'd said we'd talk about everything.

Be truthful and uninhibited.

But we couldn't talk about the future.

About a future we'd share I mean.

It was like we were uncomfortable talking about the future.

A taboo.

RAMO. They multiply. I've been thinking about it for a long time. They multiply, there're more and more of them.

Now it's those two, next it's more and more.

I stared straight at them, right at them.

And the kids laughed.

They looked at me and they laughed at me.

At a certain point, they stopped laughing and went back to going through all that shit. Leaving all that disgusting crap all over the place. I was immobile. I was paralyzed with fury.

PAMELA. That kind of thing scares me.

RAMO. What kind of thing?

PAMELA. . . . everything.

RAMO. You can't let fear get the better of you.

I thought: I will not tolerate being made fun of.

I opened my mouth and told them: I will not tolerate being made fun of.

PAMELA. And what did they do.

RAMO. They didn't look up, they kept digging in the trash. With filthy hands and the stink coming out of the bags and it was getting stronger and dispersing in the air in every direction.

PAMELA. You think he might not come at all?

RAMO. Like I said, he knew where you'd be, he knows you're here. If he doesn't come it's on purpose.

PAMELA. I'm starting to get nervous.

RAMO. "Didn't you hear me?" I shouted at them.

Is the filth blocking your ears?

Do you not understand language?

Am I not being clear?

Can you see me?

I am a clean adult, I'm standing up, right here, a few yards away and you're acting like you don't even know I'm here.

Am I here?

Look at me you human garbage. Now, when I'm talking to you, you look at me.

PAMELA. You shouldn't yell at children. They don't learn that way.

RAMO. Finally one of them looked at me, raised his head and looked at me scornfully.

I told him to apologize.

For what? he asked.

Apologize in general, I told him, for everything, apologize to me for everything.

He made a gesture I didn't understand, I'm not gonna repeat it because it was pretty obscene. I've never seen it before but it looked disgustingly crude.

So that's the way you want to do it, check out what I'm gonna do.

I took out my revolver and pointed it at him. He went still, his arms fell to the sides of his little body.

PAMELA. You had a revolver?

RAMO. I have one, I've always had a revolver.

Want to see it?

FIGURE 4.6 Cura and Krakov in Drut's Abasto production, Buenos Aires, 2013. *Photograph by Sol Pittau.*

PAMELA. No, I don't really like guns. They make me a little anxious, too . . . jumpy, I think they're weird . . .

RAMO. He came closer, he took a few little steps toward me. The other one started to insult me, defiantly, and this one was moving closer, toward the gun, toward the barrel of the gun and the other kept up the insults. Unrepeatable insults. Then he came closer to the gun, pushed his forehead to the barrel, and closed his eyes, like he was inviting me to shoot, and the other was insulting more fiercely and I didn't have any other choice but to shoot.

After the bang, the other one screamed like a pig, like pigs being slaughtered. This one had fallen at my feet, he was missing a part of his skull, it was a short distance from the other kid, I even think he might've stepped on it when he was coming toward me, that must be what he slipped on. If it wasn't on that, it was on some greasy piece of garbage, whatever, he slipped and dragged himself toward the fallen kid and touched his face and screamed louder. A horrible scream, I couldn't listen to it anymore, between the screams and the bang my ears were killing me and I thought everything was too dirty. All this was way too filthy. Nothing in the world is filthier than this thing that's been shot and the screams and the filth and I aimed at his back and I shot and shot and shot while he kept screaming and I shot again and again until he was quiet on top of the other, one on the other, and I said to them, there you go, maybe now you can learn some respect, everything is fucking impossible.

That's what I was saying as I was realizing my pants had got splashed on. Luckily I remembered I had another pair in my bag, my just-in-case pants, I always keep a spare pair in case it rains or these get wrinkled, I have a backup. I changed in the bathroom there.

5

TINO. We went in a bus, seven hours, the road was slow, it always happens on long weekends, the road gets slow, the tourists are packed in their cars on top of all the trucks. I was grossed out by those slow-motion tourists, but then I thought, we're tourists too, we're going on our vacation like everyone else. Being aware of tourism doesn't make me different from the rest.

MANU. Those trips are stressful, I prefer to stay at home, no travel.

TINO. I tell myself I'm not gonna travel anymore or at least not that kind of trip. But I always end up going. To make it worse, it was a test trip, she didn't know it but I did.

It was secret, but it was a test trip, like when NASA sends a rocket into space outside the stratosphere just to see if the cargo can survive—that's what this trip was for me. The possibilities of survival were slim.

But sometimes you bet . . . I mean you try, I mean, even up to the end you keep believing it can survive.

MANU. Sure, in the end something always survives.

TINO. We arrived at dawn, she was asleep, her mouth was open and through the window you could see the dunes, you couldn't make out the sea, it might've been too dark, but you couldn't see the sea: dunes and a few tufts of beach grass. And something glittered as the bus passed by.

She was breathing deeply in her sleep. It took me a second to realize the glimmers were from garbage, bits of plastic, glass, cans left half buried in the dunes.

I looked at her and wanted to say something. A tourist has to have a comment. She seemed to be plunging deeper and deeper into sleep, like a person drowning, no rescue, I just looked at her and thought: this won't work. This is the end. And there are four days left. I know this is over and the trip has just begun.

MANU. So you have to try to forget you know it's over, and fake this hope that doesn't exist.

TINO. Something like that. We stayed in a hotel. A horrible hotel that didn't look anything like the photos. Everything was smaller and the window looked onto a wall. We were exhausted, lay down without unpacking. We woke up after noon suffocating in the heat and flies.

And from that moment commenced the simulation.

I pronounce myself exhausted. I'm going to stay in the room. She goes to the beach to get some sun.

It starts out fake and turns real. I say the sunlight bothers me and from then on, every time I go out I feel it hurt my eyes. I see myself in the mirror, my eyes are irritated, red, they're burning. I need to keep them closed, I'm afraid I'll go blind, I'm afraid I'll never see again, never again, everything black forever.

She wants to stay with me, but I ask her to leave me alone, I don't want to ruin her vacation, she should go to the beach, get some sun, lots of sun so her skin will tan and turn red and then brown and leave me here, alone and pale. Shadow man.

She insists on staying with me, staying in the dark in the room, but in the end she gives in, lets me have my way and leaves with the blanket and an annoying basket she brought for beach things.

And I'm free in this disgusting place, listening to the tourists in the neighboring rooms.

I wait for the moments she's not there.

I don't desire her.

I say it out loud.

I have no desire.

And when I say it the bedroom becomes a tomb. I've been buried alive and nobody knows.

We go out walking at night, holding hands. On the main street.

I'm a cadaver, doesn't anyone notice I'm not alive? I'd beg for help, I'd scream if I could, I'd run away. The hand holding mine has no idea of the crisis I'm in. Doesn't know I'm mourning a death. My desire is dead. I don't love you anymore. I'm not with you. I'm not even close to myself. But I keep going—how many days do I have left? Two? One? Maybe I can do more, I might be wrong, maybe I'm not dead, just in agony, there's always hope, as tiny as it might be, there's always a sliver of hope. We grow up believing those kinds of delusions.

We sit down in a bar.

We're silent, there's not much to say.

It's not a comfortable silence. There's no closeness in it.

She asks if I like the sea.

She's asked me this question countless times.

We've been having this conversation since we met.

I think it was one of our first questions.

I say: I prefer the mountains.

She says, mountains frighten me. They give me vertigo, I feel insignificant.

I say I understand, we go back to silence.

MANU. Sometimes there are no words.

TINO. Sometimes there aren't.

You do what you can but there's nothing.

We return in silence. The whole trip, the same bus. Like we're coming back from a stranger's funeral—nobody we know, but someone who inspires respect. We don't know who's dead, but we know they must be important. That kind of silence. She falls asleep against the window. I stay awake.

MANU. I don't know what to say.

TINO. It'd be better to get out of here.

MANU. Where to?

TINO. Wherever, it'd be better than all this.

MANU. That's a pretty pessimistic idea.

TINO. Everything's going to be dark soon, any minute.

MANU. I still miss her, in my way, a little, I miss her.

TINO. I have a toothache, it's been days.

MANU. A little while before we broke up we went to a party.

TINO. I hate parties.

MANU. It was a theme party.

TINO. What kind?

MANU. We had to dress as "poor people."

Neither of us thought it sounded like much fun. At first we didn't think we were gonna go, but in the end we did.

TINO. You wind up doing things you don't want to, you don't feel like, the obligations of being a couple . . . it happens.

MANU. Maybe. The thing is we spent a whole afternoon trying on outfits that looked like poor people. We never managed it, we wanted to get to a truly realistic place.

She always had elegance. Even naked, she kept her elegance.

TINO. I can imagine.

MANU. We marked up our faces with coal but it wasn't the right effect.

She made mud and we dirtied our skin, our clothes.

We tore our clothes, we shredded them but it didn't work—poor people, the people we call poor people, we didn't look like them. But we said fine, we're something like it.

Like we referenced poorness, but we didn't look like it in itself. I don't know if you understand what I'm saying.

TINO. Sure, I can see the difference.

MANU. I mean, when you're born poor, it's no use, no matter how hard you try you can't get out of that.

TINO. You can go the opposite way.

MANU. You think so?

I'm not that sure.

We were dying of laughter when we saw what we looked like.

The mud dried on our skin, later it was cracking.

TINO. Of course, I know what mud is.

MANU. When we got to the party, we saw we'd gotten much better realism than the others. We looked much more like the concept of poverty. She was always very observant. She never lacked curiosity, it helps . . .

TINO. Tomorrow I'll go to the clinic and they'll yank out that molar. I can't tolerate the pain, it distracts me from everything.

MANU. At the party, there were appetizers made from poor peoples' ingredients. Little squares of polenta, little balls of rice with tomato, tater tots, toast with lard.

FIGURE 4.7 Señorales, Cura, Krakov, and Aramburu in Drut's Abasto production, Buenos Aires, 2013. *Photograph by Sol Pittau.*

TINO. Don't you believe that poor people eat cheaply. They eat badly, no variety, but it's not cheap.

MANU. You can learn how to eat.

You need to know how to choose, how to shop, educating your palette can take years.

TINO. I just felt a little hungry.

MANU. Something strange happened.

At the end of the party.

This is the point of the whole story.

TINO. What is?

MANU. The guests left their coats in a bedroom.

TINO. Like every party.

MANU. But in this case, the coats were hiding the poor people outfits. The coats, also some purses and wraps, a few wraps were there.

FIGURE 4.8 The red coat: Cura, Aramburu, Señorales, and Krakov in Drut's Abasto production, Buenos Aires, 2013. *Photograph by Sol Pittau.*

TINO. Coats always hide something.

MANU. When the people wanted to go home, they discovered they'd been robbed.

TINO. What? Who did it?

MANU. That was the weird thing.

None of the guests were needy people. That's why the theft seemed so strange.

TINO. What was missing?

MANU. Money out of purses, things from peoples' pockets, keychains, change.

TINO. Sometimes people steal for no reason, just to steal, no motive.

MANU. She had things missing from her purse.

She never told me what, but it seemed like they stole something valuable.

We went home in silence. She barely said a thing. One stupid sentence. I thought about that sentence for days.

TINO. Which was?

MANU. Something like: there's nothing worse than losing your trust. It wasn't that exactly. but she said something like that, quietly, I could barely hear it.

TINO. She was talking about being robbed. About thinking she was in a safe place and finding out she wasn't.

MANU. Yes, that's the obvious part, but there was a hidden meaning in that sentence. It was meant for me. It wounded me. I felt like, now I'm lost.

TINO. It's a mistake to think like that.

It was just about the clothes, the costume, the overcoats.

You were just thinking.

MANU. There was something else I keep thinking about.

The day I met her it was a red coat.

TINO. On her?

MANU. No, I was wearing a red coat.

TINO. I've never seen you in red, you're usually more dark tones, blues, blacks.

MANU. Exactly. My mother had given me a red coat as a present.

It seemed like a bad idea from the beginning. I mean wearing it. But that day I put it on.

I was uncomfortable in it. Preoccupied, thinking about people attracted by this color, staring at my clothes. When I met her, I forgot about it.

TINO. Sure, you forget.

MANU. But I never put the coat on again.

And I often think about her meeting me with the coat, the red. I mean, whether later she wished my personality, or at least my

wardrobe, had more to do with that first moment . . . I'm sure she was
disappointed.

TINO. When?

MANU. Ever since. Ever since that day. When the red went away.

That's what I thought: the first image is the one that counts, no matter how wrong.

TINO. You should stop thinking.

MANU. Can't.

TINO. You're going to explode.

MANU. It's dark out.

TINO. We should stay a little longer.

MANU. If you like.

6

TINO. Waiting is boring.

PAMELA. It sucks, I was excited.

TINO. Maybe another day.

PAMELA. Maybe.

TINO. Don't be sad.

PAMELA. I'm not sad, I'm disappointed.

TINO. Who knows, maybe you'll see him another day.

PAMELA. I'm starting to not care.

TINO. Happens sometimes.

PAMELA. Yeah, it happens, time, waiting, it all happens.

TINO. There are a lot of poor people out, don't go out alone.

They're demonstrating.

It's a mob.

PAMELA. They're not doing anything, they don't have the strength.

It's just yelling.

TINO. He'd be worried to see you alone in the streets, in the middle of that crowd.

PAMELA. I want to go somewhere with no people.

TINO. Where?

PAMELA. Last time we traveled together it was to the mountains.

TINO. Mountains make me anxious, I prefer the ocean.

PAMELA. It's not a question of preference, mountains are mountainous, you feel them. It's something past taste, it's overpowering.

TINO. Maybe, I never thought about it.

PAMELA. He fell asleep in the grass.

I went for a walk, I was distracted.

Lost in my thoughts.

I walked a long way and came to a cliff.

I could see the whole landscape from there, the wind was hitting me in the face, slapping me, insulting.

I can't describe the landscape to you, there aren't words . . . well, OK, I'll try so you can see it: mountains, and clouds, and below a wide river and swaths of land in different colors, and greenery, and stone, higher and bigger, you can't imagine how enormous.

And I thought, "I am this, and that is the landscape."

Just this.

I felt pathetic, looking at the landscape.

This smallness.

I thought, if I take one step, if I fall off this cliff with my arms open, I'll become a part of the landscape.

This is the world. What I'm looking at, this immensity, is the world.

And then I realized, I said: I am part of the world.

I have the right to be a part of it.

All of my power. This tiny power that gives me life, that gets me up every morning. This power could also be part of everything I'm looking at with these big wide eyes. My part.

My territory. And also I complete the landscape, I need that to be true. I need to belong to all that. To not be outside of it.

I am this part of that immensity, and that scares me, and it gives me life.

I declare myself a living part of the world.

I exist on this cliff.

A fervent part of the world.

I leave myself here. I root myself here. I deliver myself here.

I step forward.

  . . .

TINO. But you didn't.

PAMELA. He shouted. He called me, I turned around. He said he was scared. He got dizzy seeing me at the edge of the cliff.

TINO. He saved you.

PAMELA. I don't know.

TINO. You're here. With me, remembering all this.

PAMELA. Sometimes, during all that time, when he wasn't there yet. I could see myself falling, I had this image of my body in the void. It gave me peace. The fall. The landscape.

TINO. Better to think about something else.

PAMELA. I don't feel like thinking any more.

TINO. If you like we can leave in a bit.

I can come with you.

PAMELA. I can go alone.

TINO. Whatever you want.

PAMELA. I don't know that I want anything.

TINO. Whatever you choose will be fine.

PAMELA. Thank you.

TINO. It's not . . . I just said it to be pleasant.

PAMELA. Either way it was nice.

TINO. Thanks.

PAMELA. I'm missing so much, but I don't know what.

TINO. Everything is dark, tomorrow there may be light. Not now though, that's for sure.

PAMELA. I'm not afraid.

TINO. Better to not be.

PAMELA. Yeah, better to not be afraid.

THE END

TRANSLATOR/EDITOR'S NOTE

Altitude Sickness was commissioned by an ensemble of four young actors, a cohort Loza doesn't typically write for, and the play provides a nice illustration of the "business" side of theater pulling a writer out of his comfort zone to create new effects. As Loza notes in his interview, the play is an outlier in his *oeuvre* in a variety of ways.

Unlike most of the other plays in this book, *Altitude Sickness* is mostly dialogue (even the Father in *Winter Animals* often feels like one of Loza's monologuists, the Son commenting monosyllabically). Also in contrast to many of Loza's other works, the characters here are young and speak informally, in contemporary, colloquial language. Both elements made a nice contrast for us as translators. Loza's famous poetry is here to be found in a bum pissing on a statue and a beach littered with cigarette butts.

Both structurally and thematically, the commission also seems to have pushed Loza to a more experimental space than he often inhabits. *Winter Animals* has its tricks of time and a non-naturalistic character, but *Altitude Sickness* wears its experimentation both more subtly and more shockingly. Loza often writes characters with troubling views, for example about class, and asks us to empathize with them even as we disapprove (see Miriam in *I Was Born to See You Smile*.) Here, Loza pushes the class callousness he sees in Buenos Aires society to its shocking logical extreme, and gives us less insight into the humanity of his characters. He refuses to make them villains though, nor to make melodrama of their violence. He sites brutal acts in dramaturgically casual locations, asking us to view class cruelty with as little fuss as his characters do, proceeding as they do to engage in fractured small talk.

In the face of the tonal toughness of the play, micro-translation matters seem to pale in significance. But as always, small questions bring up big questions. To wit: Tino tells Pamela he ate a "pebete." A *pebete* is a small sandwich, or technically the fluffy white roll with which such sandwiches are made, usually filled with ham, cheese, and/or tomato. I am receptive to the argument that, like names, cultural objects like this one can be left untranslated; even that to replace such items with destination-culture equivalents may enact a kind of colonial oppression. Or I should say that I am receptive to this argument in the case of, for example, a novel, whose readership may pleasurably dwell with such a reminder of the foreignness of the story, and then peruse a footnote describing the qualities of the *pebete* in lavish detail. But as discussed, a functioning playscript does not afford that luxury. As a matter of practicality, right now the North American theater ecosystem is so hostile to work in translation that one could argue that the translator's job is simply to remove as many obstacles to production as possible.

So we sought a rough equivalent. Like any sandwich, a *pebete* connotes many things. It is mini-sublike in shape (a hoagie?), it's a thing you can grab quickly on the street (a slice?), it evokes the bland, processed food of childhood (a hot dog!). True story: we had settled on "hoagie" because it was funnier, but the act of composing this note revealed that "hot dog" ticked more boxes. Hot dog it is.

THE SAINT

A white room / GIRL is dressed in white / she could be a nurse or a nun / an elderly MAN in a wheelchair / also in white / this is the image: white.

MAN. Water—I need water thirst and water . . .

GIRL. Alright, wait.

You're not going to dry up.

MAN. Thirst and water.

Dry up.

GIRL. What do you want?

Well, let's see.

Ask the way you're supposed to, and I'll give it to you.

MAN. Water, thirst and water.

GIRL. If you drink too much, you'll pee on yourself.

And then who's going to change you?

Who's going to change you?

Let's take a guess who's going to change you.

And I changed your diaper an hour ago.

We're not going to change you every hour.

MAN. Water and thirst.

Dry up dry up dry up.

GIRL. Also if I give you water,

if you get used to drinking water nonstop, you won't make any saliva.

And then things'll get worse, if you don't make saliva you can't swallow right.

FIGURE 5.1 (PREVIOUS PAGE) Jennifer Herzog and Dean Robinson in the Cherry Artists' Collective production, Ithaca, NY, 2019. *Photograph by Sarah Chaneles.*

Your food'll get stuck in your throat.

It'll get bogged up.

And then it'll fall out.

Your food'll fall out, and who's going to clean it up?

Let's take a guess who's going to clean up the food that falls on the floor.

MAN. Dry.

Water dry water dry water.

GIRL. OK, but you're going to drink it slowly.

Let's see. There, like that, let it flow in, bit by bit, sip by sip.

Don't choke, don't drown yourself, it's only water, it's not that delicious—well, it doesn't taste bad, water's just water, and you're thirsty cause you're drying up.

Done?

You had enough?

You're hydrated?

The water I would have liked to taste is the water that flowed out at Lourdes, when the Virgin had just disappeared. A spring came up right where she'd been. That water must be special, because of what it stands for. A spring also came up where Saint Hippolyta got killed—they were about to abuse her holy body in the woods and her head got smashed on a rock and her attacker was shocked to see the martyr's blood transform into crystal-clear water, and the evildoer repented and burst into tears and bowed down and drank from the spring like a new baptism. He was absolved by God, in His infinite mercy.

The thing is, to have a martyr, you have to have an assassin.

Every saint has her corresponding sinner, you can't have one without the other, it's the spiritual ecosystem.

MAN. Holy saint saint saint.

Holy water.

Dry up and thirsty.

Thirsty holy thirsty holy saint saint saint.

GIRL. Peace.

I need peace.

I'm burning up inside.

All this quiet and I'm burning.

My senses are all confused.

I try but I can't manage, I can't feel complete.

Calm is always escaping me.

MAN. Peace.

Cease peace.

Dry up.

Home.

Oh how lovely.

GIRL. I have my calling.

For example, now I pick up this rag, I squeeze it,

And that has something to do with my calling.

Give, give, give. My vocation is about offering up.

I've known since I was a girl.

I was called.

He called me.

In his way.

I still listen to Him.

My first memory is of church.

The first time my soul vibrated.

I was looking at the cupola.

I pressed my hands together and I said to myself.

FIGURE 5.2 Valeria Lois, directed by Lisandro Rodriguez at the Elefante Club de Teatro, Buenos Aires, Argentina, 2011. *Photograph by Nora Lezano.*

I'm going to be a saint.

One way or another.

I'm going to give myself up to God.

I said that to God.

I said it to Him just like I was saying it to you.

Lord, I am not worthy that you enter my house,

But one word of yours will be enough to heal me.

I can make this easier, not so much theory.

I said to him: Lord, I am an innocent girl, I know barely anything about life, nor about the world.

I am not very intelligent, nor very beautiful, nor very charming.

Just, I am an ordinary girl, the kind of girl nobody notices. A girl in the crowd, one more, like you can separate girls into the ones who stand out in front and the ones at the back. I am a girl at the back, not outstanding.

Lord, if you call me, if you let me come to you, I shall move out of the shadows, I shall clothe myself in Grace.

Lord, here is my life, I offer it to you to do what you please with it.

Lord, are you listening?

Lord I beg you.

Take me far away, kidnap me, get me out of this filthy place, grab me, kill me, annihilate me, make me dust, pulverize me, make me good.

MAN. Seltzer.

Pelt her.

Pelt.

GIRL. Seltzer is disgusting.

All those bubbles puffing you up.

I don't agree with seltzer.

When I was a girl, I was playing in the yard.

I was chasing a dove, I thought maybe it was the Holy Spirit made manifest, I was running after it asking, "Are you the Spirit or not? Come on, be revealed!" The dove had a crippled wing, he was a little busted-down you could say, and he was doing these short little hops. I was so focused on the dove I didn't see anything else, and when I followed him into the alley I didn't notice a couple of crates of seltzer right in the middle. I tripped, and fell on top of them and all the bottles exploded. Pieces of glass shot into my legs, and blood sprang up. At first I screamed. But then right away I fell silent. I thought: this is a trial God is sending me, I have to bear the pain so the dove will reveal himself. I allowed the blood to flow out, I wanted all the blood

out, to purify me. The dove watched the blood come out of me.
Motionless. Till I suddenly passed out.

Everything went white.

I woke up in the hospital with my father at my side, he was crying. He asked me: Are you alright? I had no strength.

My mother wasn't there.

From the beginning, she wasn't there.

She'd never been there.

She died in childbirth.

I killed my mother.

The day I was born, my mother died.

Nobody knew whether to be happy or the opposite.

Simultaneous, me born her dead.

Like people who pass each other in the street without meeting, it was like that, my mother and I passed each other. We never saw each other, no contact.

Everything happened in the same hospital.

That same hospital where I'm waking up now, and seeing my father crying.

Are you OK?, he asks me.

Of course.

Purified, I'm thinking.

The exploded bottles, encrusted in my body, reaching the center of my flesh.

Don't move, my father says, you're sewn up all over the place. They sewed you up like a stuffed pork.

The stitches pull.

Still. It's been years and I can still feel the sewing in my skin.

I've cut myself other times since then, and they've sewn me up. I'm all patchwork.

MAN. Evil.

Pelt seltzer.

Evil.

The wind.

GIRL. Do you think it's raining?

You think it's raining outside?

I don't think so.

I think we'd hear it.

Not even the rain.

Nothing.

Are you feeling alright?

Do you feel like sleeping?

I'm always sleepy.

I struggle with that.

I fight to stay awake.

If I didn't make an effort, I'd just sleep.

A whole life asleep.

I get drowsy when I pray.

That's why I make such an effort.

Ever since I was a girl.

I'd concentrate when I prayed. So I wouldn't fall asleep.

I'd squeeze the rosary very tight. I pushed every bead. One by one. A thousand times.

FIGURE 5.3 (FACING PAGE) Herzog in the Cherry Artists' Collective production, Ithaca, NY, 2019. *Photograph by Sarah Chaneles.*

I prayed a lot. Voraciously. I prayed like it was a vice. I passed the beads again and again. Mystery after mystery. I prayed and passed the beads. I destroyed those beads. With the strength of my prayer, the force. I wore the beads out with the push of my fingers, they were wooden beads and they flattened, they wound up like lentils. I smushed them.

I was waiting for an apparition.

I always knew I would be a saint.

But a saint can't be sure about her sainthood until she has her own apparition.

I never got one.

I was denied.

For years.

I don't ask for many things. But I did ask for that, a manifestation.

God could have been a little more generous about that.

Maybe I didn't deserve it.

You can't know.

God has a strange way of thinking, it doesn't have our same logic.

MAN. The wind.

The wind.

You're evil.

All evil.

GIRL. Does it hurt you here?

If your knee hurts, it's definitely raining.

When you get a pain in your knee, it's going to be a long shower.

When it rains, the smell of disinfectant goes away.

Gets neutralized.

You all have that smell, same smell as the sheets, the floors, the hallways.

Everything smells the same.

At night when I bathe, I rub myself good and strong with soap, to get the smell off, so it doesn't stick to me.

Not yet.

I'm young.

I always washed myself a lot.

There's no sin in cleaning yourself.

You can be as naked as anything, but washing yourself is not a sin.

I always felt dirty.

Since the day I was born.

Like my baptism didn't clean out all my original sin, like a little stayed stuck to me, and I need to get it off. Every day I try to get it off, but it's an oily kind of dirtiness that never comes off completely.

Never.

My aunt used to say to me: you're a sow. You're a dirty girl.

My aunt raised me when my father couldn't anymore.

What's a sow? I asked her.

A sow is a female pig.

A sow is a pig.

I'm a pig.

I'm dirty.

We prayed a lot with my aunt.

Pray, she told me, pray a lot and find out if God will forgive you.

You arrived stained, from the beginning, when you came in like a savage and shoved your mother out.

You're here because she's gone, that's what she said.

So we would pray for hours.

On our knees. Until our legs fell asleep.

You have to bear that numbness in your legs.

Stop feeling, or feel without feeling, like amputees feel.

If only I'd even had that bit of luck, to be deformed, handicapped, to have some visible thing to offer up. But the marks I have aren't visible, they're nothing to the Lord. Just internal scars.

Everything is bleeding, but on the inside.

Men don't know anything about blood.

We know.

I asked my aunt about that when I got it, and she explained. I asked if the Virgin Mary menstruated too. Boy, she whacked me one. My cheek was red for ages.

That's how I found out it's better not to ask.

There are things you don't question.

You have to accept, just accept without asking.

And I accept the will of the Lord, even though I don't know what it is, I still don't know what He has prepared for me.

MAN. Evil evil.

Evil queen.

Evil dirty.

GIRL. Be quiet! Be quiet or we're not gonna get along.

If you get aggressive, I'll give you the pill and you'll go to sleep and that's it for our walk.

We'll button up buttercup, and you'll sleep until tomorrow.

And tomorrow?

What's the point in waking up tomorrow.

. . .

There was a silly little saint, I always adored him, little San Eugenio de Palomba.

He wasn't smart, he didn't talk very much and what he said he said wrong, he didn't have very much vocabulary, I mean it wasn't only that, more like he didn't have very much control and he drooled a little when he spoke words.

He worked in a convent, he didn't have religious training, his job was cleaning the sacristy, the bathrooms, the storerooms. He'd been left there in a basket when he was just born. Poor little tyke, the monks

FIGURE 5.4 Jennifer Herzog and Dean Robinson in the Cherry Artists' Collective production, Ithaca, NY, 2019. *Photograph by Sarah Chaneles.*

fed him and educated him, but he never learned very much. He mostly just cleaned while the monks chanted.

And that's the funny thing. At dawn one day while he was cleaning, Christ appears to little Eugenio, in spirit and in flesh, and not only Christ himself (and that would have been enough), but the Sacred Heart. Which is Christ with his heart open and lit up. Beautiful like a painting. Unbelievable.

I was so happy when I learned the story of little San Eugenio, I loved to think of how long the monks would have to wait to see Christ, and He goes and shows himself to the cleaning staff.

Because He prefers the meek, the modest, the weak ones, to call to in whatever way.

That poor little saint couldn't really even understand the messages Christ was telling him. But the Lord is patient about that, Christ repeated things several times so little Eugenio could understand them.

It's a beautiful story, the little saint. He is represented with a feather duster and an expression of simplicity. More than simplicity, vacancy. When I saw the statue, I thought he had the same look on his face that cows do.

All statues have a strange look in their eyes, but his is stranger.

I always thought that must be it.

My lack of simplicity.

God doesn't like me complicated and I know that at any moment I'll have messed it all up. Lost myself.

Lord, I am lost.

Give me a path so I can follow you.

MAN. Water water.

GIRL. You're just being spoiled.

You can't be thirsty, you just had a drink.

You can't be thirsty if you're not doing anything.

You haven't sweated, or peed, or cried, or done anything at all to dry you up.

You haven't done a thing, not even listened.

Doing nothing.

Just an idler.

Completely lazy.

You're all idlers, that's what my aunt would say to my cousins.

Idlers and sinners.

Laziness is an unforgivable sin, she said.

As if that mattered to them. They didn't even pay attention.

Especially the ones on the ends, the biggest and the smallest. The middle one was different.

His name was Mariano. Because he wasn't a girl and my aunt couldn't call him Maria like she wanted. God gave her three sons, no daughters, that's why she raised me.

The oldest was named José, after the Virgin Mary's husband, the youngest was Jeremias from the Bible (I forget who he was), the middle one was Mariano, like I told you. Later she had two more, but they died young, one when he was born and the other after a month, suffocated on his pillow. Sometimes it's hard to understand why God does that kind of thing. Why he sends sons to live such a short time. Maybe so there can be a limbo, so the place for young souls won't be empty, I don't know, I'm only guessing, I don't want to question what God decides, of course God must know what he's doing. The thing is my aunt only had three sons, none of the daughters she wanted. Well, yes, she had me, but it wasn't the same.

The two on the ends, the oldest and the youngest, would show me their penis when my aunt wasn't looking. It made me feel curious and also disgusted. Not the middle one. Mariano was always more modest.

The other two were always touching themselves. Disgusting.

Like animals in heat.

Always with erections.

Not Mariano, he was very quiet.

My father would leave me at my aunt's house for weeks, sometimes he forgot to come pick me up.

My aunt was strict. That was hard, but she was also very devout and I liked that.

To have faith, you have to have discipline.

I learned that from her.

I didn't have very much.

FIGURE 5.5 Herzog and Robinson in the Cherry Artists' Collective production, Ithaca, NY, 2019. *Photograph by Sarah Chaneles.*

It's about then, when my cousins and I were young, that the light bulb thing happened.

The rumor spread like a tornado.

Miracles were happening in our town.

It was kind of an open secret.

It'd happen when a light bulb burned out.

They said when they burned out, an impression got made inside the glass, out of the exact center of the vacuum, of a perfect cross.

It had already happened a few times.

One time it happened to the young priest who was in charge of the parish on weekends. He only had one eye, and he stuttered, and one night it happened to him. He didn't tell anyone except the woman who cleaned the chapel, and she spread it around everywhere. The other person it happened to was Mrs. Matilde. This rich lady from the city who had married the mayor. Neither Mrs. Matilde nor the young priest acknowledged the miracle had happened to them. They pretended to be all mysterious. And there's nothing worse than a miracle that doesn't get shared. A gesture from God is nothing to be stingy about.

The idea of having a miracle at home had me quivering all day. I prayed for a bulb to burn out, I'd turn the lights on and off to see if the blinking would burn one out.

All day waiting for night, to turn on the bulbs. As soon as one burned out, I'd call my aunt to change it, and she'd unscrew it, trembling, and look at it and be disappointed there was no miracle.

Mariano was waiting as well. He had the calling too. Not like the others, showing their penises at the smallest excuse.

Since there was no miracle at home, my aunt went on a campaign to see the lucky bulbs, Mrs. Matilde's and the young priest's.

It turned out the young priest couldn't be bribed. My aunt gave him four jars of homemade fig jam, knitted a red scarf, and a few weeks later sent two boxes of cotton briefs, but she didn't get anywhere. The young priest said thank you for the presents but he kept the miracle to himself. He denied having the bulb.

But Mrs. Matilde could be. It took a long time but she could.

My aunt worked like a dog.

She was selling information. One snip of gossip after another.

Whatever would help Mrs. Matilda support the Mayor. All the rumors about conspiracies, enmities, things like that. I'm not too sure what she told her, but my aunt was very observant, and very devout, which Mrs. Matilde was as well, so they'd meet at the chapel to pray for a bit and then stay in the park, smoking cigarettes and talking.

So one day my aunt came back, very excited with the news that Mrs. Matilda was waiting for us to show us the miracle.

She combed my cousins' hair with gel and dressed them in their Sunday clothes. She braided my hair. She'd made me a pink dress with pale blue lace, it looked so beautiful on me. It made me look special.

That evening we went to the mayor's house.

The biggest house in town, with lots of plants at the door and statues of swans as big as me. I thought they looked enormous.

Mrs. Matilde brought us scones her maid had baked, she said she'd given her an English recipe because those darkies can't cook a thing if it's not stew and my aunt laughed. (I didn't really get the joke because Matilde's maid wasn't that dark, more like light brown. She was the mother of a classmate of mine who had freckles and cried a lot.)

Mrs. Matilda's living room was beautiful. There was a glass chandelier on the ceiling. While Mrs. Matilda and my aunt were talking, I looked at the drops of glass on the chandelier, the beads, like a rainfall frozen in space . . . I fell in love with that chandelier, I thought they were only in movies. And some armchairs, you sank right down to the bottom, with embroidered pillows, so beautiful. The two on the ends didn't like to stay still and they wiggled their legs and scratched, and made noises with their mouths when they drank their tea. Mariano behaved. He was even more eager to see the bulb than I was.

My aunt and Mrs. Matilde talked a blue streak and didn't even notice it was getting dark. I let them know. I told them.

It was getting dark.

Dark.

Don't be rude, my aunt said, you don't speak when adults are talking.

It was dark.

It's alright, Mrs. Matilde said and she turned on the chandelier and all the pieces of glass sparkled. I looked up at it and I fell spellbound.

Mrs. Matilde went somewhere else in the house.

You be grateful we're here or I'll give your face a slap, my aunt said. I said I was sorry for talking about the dark.

Her face was tight, she was so angry the corners of her mouth turned down. But when she heard Mrs. Matilde coming back, she arranged her expression into a kind of smile.

Suddenly there was silence.

Not that there was noise before.

I don't remember what there was before.

But now there was silence.

We didn't pay attention to Mrs. Matilde coming in, all we could see was that red case. Like a jewelry box.

And Mrs. Matilde said proudly, mysteriously, Here it is.

And stopped in front of the armchair. My aunt gestured to the four of us. My cousins and me.

The ones on the ends pretended to be well-behaved. Mariano and I understood right away.

We all got on our knees while Matilde opened the red case.

Slowly. Very slowly she uncovered what was inside.

It was full of cotton balls and in the middle of that delicate protection, there was the light bulb.

You could see the cross. It wasn't a very strong line, more smoky.

But it was definitely a cross.

My aunt started to cry.

Matilde put the little box on the coffee table and knelt down as well.

My aunt reached out her hands and squeezed me tight, and squeezed Mariano with the other hand, the others held on too and Matilda too. And we prayed a rosary right there. The whole rosary used to bore me to death, but this time it flew out of me. I was next to a miracle. It didn't happen to me, it happened to someone else. And not a very great miracle, I thought, but a miracle all the same.

A few days later, the fat man at the hardware store said there'd been a shipment of faulty light bulbs, that General Electric had issued an apology because they burned out right away and the filament left a dark mark on the glass.

My aunt preferred to not hear it.

Faith and science sometimes contradict each other.

They refute each other. They fight.

To believe you have to close your ears, if you listen to everything everyone says you can't believe anymore.

If you follow logic there are no miracles.

I was never that interested in logic.

Everything is a lie.

Oof.

Everything went dark.

For a moment.

Dark.

MAN. Dark, dark.

Night dark.

I'm sleepy.

Dark.

Night.

GIRL. Now you want to sleep?

Just when you were starting to keep me company.

That's not good.

Don't leave me now.

God, don't leave me now.

I wonder if God is his first name or last name. We don't say Mr. God. We just say God. Like we were close friends with him.

FIGURE 5.6 Herzog in the Cherry Artists' Collective production, Ithaca, NY, 2019. *Photograph by Sarah Chaneles.*

Like he wasn't intimidating. I call everybody Mr. and Mrs., but I can call him God. Like he was my friend.

MAN. Night, night.

Queen.

Night.

GIRL. Don't leave me.

Don't abandon me now.

I still have to cross the darkest part of the path.

For God's sake don't leave me.

Not now.

Then everything else happened.

Growth.

Faith.

Still, faith.

Lord, I am your unpassionate lover.

Your possible lover.

Please don't leave me.

Then I got bigger.

I was about twelve, a little older.

Mariano said that in the chapel, when he went with the Boy Scouts to confess, he had seen the eyes of the statue of the Virgin bleeding.

I'm sure he said it to please me.

I didn't see it.

At least, not with these eyes.

I spent hours staring at the statue.

But I didn't see anything bleed.

You can see things with the eyes of the soul.

Strange things happen. But physical eyes see what they see.

I didn't see it.

Mariano was interested in spiritual things, not like his brothers who were interested in other kinds of things. They wanted to know how women worked and things like that.

Not Mariano. He thought about eternal life and transcendence.

For example he was concerned about the destiny of souls.

"When we get to Heaven, the soul separates from the body. So we won't have a brain."

"So what, Mariano?"

"The brain is where intelligence lives," he said, "so we're going to be souls contemplating God with no intelligence, do you see?" he said to me, "Idiot souls . . . "

That must be the only kind of soul who can tolerate eternal life, I said.

... that's the kind of thing Mariano thought about. Theology.

"If you commit a sin and confess it, but deep down you don't repent, will God forgive it or not?"

Mariano, I don't think God forgives sins you haven't repented.

"And what if you enjoy the sin?"

"Because the sin includes pleasure?"

Don't mix me up Mariano, I don't know.

Pray, lower your eyes and be quiet.

MAN. Food, sleep, hunger, night, queen.

Owl.

GIRL. My aunt would also say I had eyes like an owl.

She'd tell me to lower my eyes, not to gawk at her.

She didn't like my way of looking.

Back then I used to look without blinking.

I'd lock my eyes onto people.

Over time, I made myself harder to find.

I used to look more than I was supposed to.

Not anymore. Now it's almost the opposite.

My view's closed up.

I see a little slice of space.

I limit myself.

I knew that life at my aunt's had a limit.

One day, my father didn't come to pick me up anymore.

I was about fifteen.

Fifteen years old with no quinceañera and no miracle.

Trying to hear what God had to say to me, and nothing from Him.

Him and Nothing.

THE SAINT

FIGURE 5.7 Lois in the Elefante production, Buenos Aires, 2011. *Photograph by Nora Lezano.*

Sometimes I think they're the same thing.

Sorry for the blasphemy.

God and nothing.

Mr. God and nothing.

Deliver me up to nothingness. Sink me inside of your immensity.

I had to deliver myself up, I believed that.

My body had to disappear.

I believe in nothingness.

My being.

If I made myself nothing I would enter into God.

That's why I went one afternoon.

Not too far.

I went to the highway.

Where the truck drivers are.

Near the gas station.

At the side of the road.

Where the night girls walked.

I'd seen them. Around then the brothers on the ends, the oldest and the youngest, used to go there to get relief. Not Mariano.

There were so many trucks coming from so many places the women couldn't keep up. There were only about ten of them. They'd hop from one cab to the next, doing fifteen minute shifts so they could take care of everybody.

The men came from all ends of the earth, you know? Some of them driving for days, far from their wives, with this unbearable pressure.

I had to offer myself up.

The offering of my body would be my bridge to holiness.

The first cab I went into smelled like wheat. I asked what he was carrying but the man didn't answer. He threw me on a mat he kept in the upper section. There wasn't much space and I couldn't breathe very well. The mat was stained, I could see that, and the man had a tattoo of a football-team logo. He weighed a lot. He had a thick smell and breathed heavy like he was going to die. I thought he was going to die on top of me and I'd be crushed trying to survive, trying to get out from under that slack body. I was afraid, but my fear gave way to a pain that tore me in two. The pain rose up from below and exploded in my head, like a lightning bolt through my whole body that crashed into the top of my head. The last thing I managed to see was the ornament that hung from the rearview mirror, a pink bootie, sort of very old, from some long-ago baby. Then I screamed and didn't see anything else, everything went black. I managed to think, here comes

God to take me. I waited for the tunnel of light and song of the angels but it stayed black. Very black. Like a hole where you never stop falling.

When I woke up I was surrounded by girls. The night girls who lived near the highway, all together in the green house.

I was burning with fever. I was on fire.

The girls took care of me. They gave me ice-water baths. They'd do their shifts and the one who wasn't working would stay with me.

I pushed, from inside my fever, to see if Christ would manifest himself in my delirium, but nothing.

Nothing. Once again. Nothing.

Over the days I started to get better.

I came back.

I'm grateful to the night girls.

I'll never forget them.

They were a good team.

They worked together, they complemented each other.

They had to soothe all those men.

And they knew how to do it.

Behind the green house, there were two little rooms and outside, some little tables to have a drink.

The little rooms were for the ones who came on foot. Or the ones who wanted to be away from the truck for a bit, or the ones from town who were taking a little walk.

Like the ones on the ends. They came every so often.

In time I got to know the job.

I was good at it, I stood out.

When the ones on the ends came, I didn't even look at them.

I pretended it was nothing.

I took care of them one after the other like I didn't know them.

I don't even think they noticed. They didn't recognize me.

When men have that need, they don't even look at the woman who's taking care of them.

The only one I couldn't was with my father.

The day he came I hid. I asked one of the girls to take care of it.

Luckily he left quickly, staying pretty much out of sight, and didn't come back while I was there.

Maybe someone told him I was there, maybe, I mean . . . maybe things like that just aren't said, I don't know . . . oh God . . .

I gave but I didn't feel pleasure. That's how I kept myself pure.

I was like the Blessed Virgin that way.

That's how I understood her, it wasn't that she never knew a man, it was that she didn't take pleasure and that kept her pure. For centuries.

Like I kept myself.

Pure and chaste.

I erased myself.

I went to nature.

Physicality decaying.

Detritus.

I knew how to touch them so they'd go fast and free up the little rooms.

They'd end up tender and harmless, like newborns.

For how strong they seem at the beginning they're vulnerable when they fall.

You feel sorry for them. In that sense, the woman is stronger.

She gets up from the bed and keeps going.

The hardest thing for me was the drinking.

The more we drank, the more they drank.

We had to make them buy us drinks.

So they'd waste money on cheap drinks that cost a fortune.

I never liked that trick.

I never liked alcohol, it's very strong.

Not even at Mass, when the priest dipped the host in wine, even though it was the blood of Christ I didn't like it at all.

Not even birthday cakes with brandy, I liked them dry. Very dry and sweet.

But there you had to get them to drink.

It's the hardest part of the job.

Dear God, if you give me this test, I will pass it triumphantly.

If I must be burned in this fire, I will burn myself and purify myself.

And I drank and drank.

La Mamita was the one who took care of us and was always tender with us. La Mamita was tired of being with men, and they didn't look at her that much. She was pretty old, when she was young she was friends with Mrs. Matilde, she told me one night while we were drinking tea.

The thing is, La Mamita helped with the dizziness.

She'd put her fingers in our throats so we'd throw up and could keep going.

Because you can't lose control. Or the man will do whatever he wants. They see you half-silly and take advantage and turn into savage animals.

The night girls called me "the Saint".

I kind of liked it, I asked them not to call me that, but inside I was flattered.

I used to convert people.

Not so many, a few, but it happened.

I'd listen to the men's problems.

FIGURE 5.8 Herzog and Robinson in the Cherry Artists' Collective production, Ithaca, NY, 2019. *Photograph by Sarah Chaneles.*

Sometimes they liked that more than the other stuff.

I was good at lending an ear.

And it wasn't so rare, when the thing was done, we'd kneel by the bed and say a prayer.

La Mamita got annoyed because if we prayed the whole rosary it took a long time and there were only two rooms which weren't enough for all the demand.

But that was my mission.

My divine path.

Your will my lord.

I am yours.

I died in every body.

I break myself and share myself among the people.

This is my body.

Eat of me.

This is my blood.

Drink until you are slaked.

Lord make of me an instrument of your love.

MAN. Evil.

Sow evil.

Night thirsty.

Time.

GIRL. I'm tired of doing all the talking.

You have no idea how exhausting it is.

That. Opening your legs and moving and waiting.

You don't know that confusion of smells, those wet sheets, that tangle of blankets, all that hair and spit all around you and the few minutes you have to get the thing done and then fix it all again to hide what the last one left behind.

But the little rooms are better than the trucks. I was firm about that, I didn't do truck cabins anymore. I'd rather stay quiet and pray.

For everything to be over.

Soon.

Diaphanous.

Chaste.

I want to be transparent.

In order to rise up, first you have to have to plunge down, like a punch to the guts of the world.

Fall, to be launched up.

To ascend like the sweet Virgin and baby Jesus.

To rise slowly into the clouds.

I knew it, I'd always known it.

I had lovely times in the green house.

The night girls have a strange purity.

A lot of tenderness too.

Ugly things happened too.

Like the one that made me run.

I would have stayed forever.

Like Saint Magdalene who calmed the ardors of Christ.

I would have stayed.

But Mariano came looking for me.

So I ran.

My legs shook when I saw him come in.

My skirt was very short, like to here.

Everyone could see my legs shaking.

He said in my ear, I came to get you.

I can't talk here, I said.

Make an appointment.

He talked to La Mamita and made one.

We went to the room.

We'd barely entered when he slapped me. It still hurts, here.

You're lost, he said. You're a terrible person.

Come with me, pig.

I'm not going anywhere, Mariano, you're not nice anymore.

He threw me on the bed.

Got on me.

I told him not to do it.

But he kept going.

He covered my face with the pillow.

I could barely breathe.

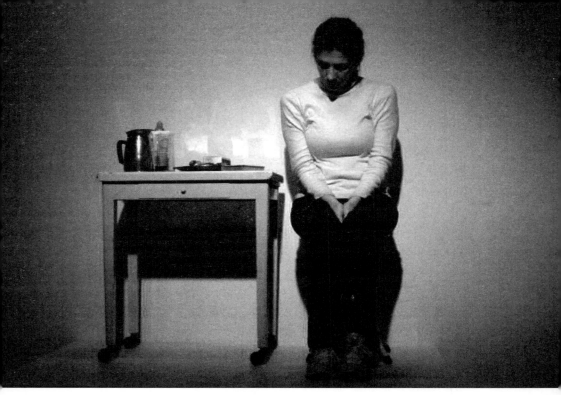

FIGURE 5.9 Lois in the Elefante production, Buenos Aires, 2011. *Photograph by Nora Lezano.*

And right there he did the same as everyone.

I went away in my mind.

Far away.

I begged God to take me away from everywhere.

I want to go away from the world.

For me, Mariano was the last good person.

God spared Sodom because one good person was there.

Mariano.

But now he was the same.

There are no good people.

There isn't anything.

Let your rain of fire and fury be delivered upon all sinners.

He took the pillow off my face and kissed me on the mouth.

I could move a little.

I moved to the side as much as I could.

I looked at him like I'd look at any man. Mariano had become a man like all the others. That's how I saw him. His whole body a man's, so sad.

I said, I'm going to pray for you not to go to hell.

He pulled up his pants and stared at me.

I was terrified.

I thought.

God, let everything end.

Make me a martyr.

He came closer, I opened my arms because I thought he wanted to hug me and I still believed in forgiveness and right then he punches me, here. I break like a reed and fall and hit my head and La Mamita knocks on the door and says Open up! and yells, What the hell is going on?

And right there, in that moment, I felt that God was asking me to stay.

Here, alive in this world.

That it wasn't time to go.

I got to my feet as well as I could.

He looked at me and you could tell he was frightened too.

The kind of fear you have of your own being.

He was afraid of himself.

And for that last moment I could see the frightened kid of the past before he was buried in the hard body of the man.

I opened the door.

I flew out of there.

I could hear them shouting for me.

Everybody.

All shouting.

The whole world shouting.

And I ran.

Barefoot.

Through the empty fields.

I ran without turning around.

Escaping like Abraham from the flames of the corrupt cities.

Far from Gomorrah.

I ran without looking back.

Lot's wife turned, and God punished her by turning her into a pillar of salt.

God punishes the curiosity of women.

I ran without turning, no curiosity, running on pure fear.

God has a bad temper. That's why he punishes so often.

I got to the highway.

A truck driver helped me.

The solidarity of the highway.

Just like the first one initiated me, the last one saved me.

The first one dirties you and the last one cleans.

That's divine law.

Anyway, we travelled three days to the city.

Almost without talking.

He took me away from all that.

I took care of him seven times. He didn't ask, but that seemed fair to me, the least I could do to be rescued.

FIGURE 5.10 Herzog and Robinson in the Cherry Artists' Collective production, Ithaca, NY, 2019. *Photograph by Sarah Chaneles*.

When we got there, I didn't even look at the lights and the buildings.

I was so tired that even though I'd lived my whole life in a little village, I wasn't interested in all that. Didn't care. I just wanted to sleep and sleep.

He brought me to the sweet nuns.

The old folks' home.

They were good to me.

They gave me a little room and a job.

Food and work.

I don't need anything else.

MAN. Food.

Night.

Food.

Hungry thirsty.

Food.

GIRL. Shhhh. We're almost there.

Soon we'll go to sleep.

Eternal sleep awaits us.

MAN. Sleepy.

Hungry.

Earth.

GIRL. Everything is useful.

Even the past.

I like to be useful.

Lots of saints were servants.

Also I'm near the nuns and they have a direct connection.

They know.

Even what came before is useful.

Make up a bed quickly.

Don't leave a trace.

And anyway, old folks don't last long.

You have to bathe them, clean them, talk to them like you talk to plants to keep them alive.

For a few months or years but in the end they go.

Like the clients at the green house, better to not feel tenderness.

Just mercy.

Even the little tricks from my last job are useful.

Sometimes an old guy needs relief and I do him one last favor.

I feel so bad for them, I mean, it's easy.

You can't know the intimate life of saints.

The things they did or didn't do.

The intimacy.

I had intimacy with Mariano. That's why I left.

We both wanted to be saints and he betrayed me.

His animal part.

The worst part.

I stayed immaculate.

Now I'm clean again.

That much pain purifies.

I'm pure.

All for God.

Even though God, you don't seem to notice me.

You keep avoiding me.

Maybe I don't seem like much to you.

Insignificant.

An insect in the immensity of the universe.

Me. Who lives and dies for you.

I give all of myself.

I shared myself to as many bodies as I could.

I was generous.

I destroyed myself.

I am demolished.

What more do you want?

What else do I have to give you?

I gave you my entire life . . .

I gave to you, I gave to you, through pain, through death I gave . . .

FIGURE 5.11 Herzog and Robinson (background) in the Cherry Artists' Collective production, Ithaca, NY, 2019. *Photograph by Sarah Chaneles.*

What more do you want?

Look at me.

Look at the misery I've become.

How far can a body go.

Is there a limit?

I don't have one.

I am infinite.

Look at me.

What else do you want?!

It's not enough for you.

Look at how I bleed, look at how I open my flesh and bleed away for you.

I am made entirely of you.

Of you and your silence.

She falls to the floor / she is bleeding from open stigmata / the MAN rises to his feet assuming the shape of a dark priest / it's one second / everything changes / he places his hand on her forehead as she convulses

MAN. Spirit of darkness, free this creature.

Evil of evils leave this place.

May all be as it was in the beginning.

God expel the evil that resides in this wounded body.

Forgive her offenses.

Drive out the darkness.

Lord of Night leave from within this place.

Abandon this human creature.

Give her peace.

Now.

And for centuries of centuries.

May it be so.

He sits back down in the wheelchair / bit by bit she comes back / as if liberated from a terrible battle / she returns exhausted
Silence.

GIRL. I'm back.

You're a beautiful man.

Very beautiful.

I'm so tired.

Thank you for waiting for me.

I'm calm now.

This purity . . .

This kind of holiness that's come down upon me . . .

Something beautiful happened.

The place I went, God was there.

He was short.

Blond.

Such bright eyes.

He was holding this smaller guy's hand and they were laughing a lot.

Both of them.

They wanted to cross the street.

There was a lot of traffic.

I took God's hand. I walked Him right between the cars.

When we got to the other side, he looked at me and said: We're safe. It's a miracle.

I thought so too. Safe, I repeated.

I kissed him on the forehead.

I told him to take care.

He winked at me and walked away with the little guy.

I've seen God.

I saw God and I wasn't afraid.

I'm not afraid.

No fear at all.

Nothing.

MAN. Water.

Water.

Sleep.

GIRL. Yes. Yes, we'll go to sleep soon.

So soon.

Eternal rest.

THE END

TRANSLATOR/EDITOR'S NOTE[1]

As I write this note, *La mujer puerca* is, amazingly, still running in its eighth season in Buenos Aires, still starring the incredible Valeria Lois in the Girl's now-iconic pink turtleneck and lip gloss. Prospective performers of this text in English should note that as Lois performs her, the Girl is anything but self-pitying: the actress is famously comic, and the Girl often seems to embody an almost absurd and heartbreakingly funny impulse to look on the bright side.

On the micro-technical level I love to explore, in this play Ariel and I solved two quintessential Spanish translation challenges with one choice. The Girl at one point muses about why God is addressed in the informal "vos" rather than the formal "usted," a distinction we don't have in English; elsewhere, she refers to her mother's higher-class friend as "la Matilde." We were pleased with the idea that she might call Matilde "Mrs. Matilde," resonating with historic English working-class address, and it set us up nicely for her to wonder why we don't say "Mr. God."

In a very different way from *Winter Animals*, *La mujer puerca* also tested our ability to translate a title. Indeed it is almost comical to imagine how *La mujer puerca* could possibly be best translated as *The Saint*. What's worse, I have no more specific reason for our title problematic than the strong feeling that *The Pig Woman* is not a great title in English, and that a great play should have a great title.

When I brought this notion up with Loza, he was untroubled. (Playwrights in Argentina are accustomed to having their texts adjusted by directors; more on that later.) He told us that up until late in its development, one of the play's working titles was *La santa*. There being no English word for a specifically female saint, *The Saint* is a flawed translation of this too. On the other hand, most of Loza's titles are pulled from the play texts, and part of their function emerges as the kind of "click" happens when the title is spoken in the play. (See *I Was Born to See You Smile* and *Nothing to Do with Love* [*Makes Me*

---

1 The translators would like to thank Natalia Fernández Acquier, whose supertitle translation provided a helpful jumping-off point for this performance translation.

Envious]). We found that in English, the way *The Saint* reveals itself in the text was lovely enough to give it the clear edge over *The Pig Woman*.

*

My many adventures with international plays have taught me that anybody in the English-speaking world working with these texts is well-advised to consider the cultural differences in the job descriptions of director and playwright (when these descriptors even apply.) Germany provides the name and most prominent tradition of the *Regietheater*, in which the director may radically reshape the text; the Anglo theater occupies the most extreme opposite position, in which the text is sacrosanct and a director's job is often described as simply to create an embodiment of the playwright's vision. Most theater traditions in Latin America and Europe, while not as extreme as the German one, are also not as extreme as ours, and expect the director to take some level of authorial power—which in turn affects how playwrights write.

This phenomenon became vivid in our work on *The Saint*. I was introduced to *La mujer puerca* by attending the Buenos Aires production and reading the text as it had been translated for supertitles. When the play was published in Loza's *Textos Reunidos*, I was startled to meet for the first time the character of the old Man. The director of the Buenos Aires production had cut the character: after rehearsing with two actors for a time, the team decided the Man didn't work. In that still-running production, the Girl speaks to the audience, who she has greeted as they enter the theater.

The show has been running for enough years to establish that this directorial emendation created a highly effective evening of theater. Nonetheless, I find the play more satisfying with the Man in it. (Without him, we start in a vivid but odd media res: "The water I would like to have tried was . . . "; and we end with an uncontextualized voice from the void.) When the Cherry Artists' Collective produced the play in 2019, we were pleased to be the first production to include both characters.

Needless to say, he makes for a very different show! Our production team also found that it was strange to have the Girl talk to a silent man (one kept wondering if he had already died), so the actor often responded to her with inchoate sounds that occasionally formed themselves into the semi-intelligible lines on the page. The relationship added a significant interest and dynamic to the play that the Buenos Aires production, of course, could not have (at the end, is she putting something in his water?) And in a sense it was a good thing that it did: in shifting the play from its highly Catholic Argentine audience to our largely secular North American one, while the pathos of the story remained intact, much of the humor of the Girl's cockeyed view of Catholicism was lost.

At a talkback after the Cherry production, Loza was asked what he thought about seeing the play for the first time with the Man in it. He confessed that like most artists he is often insecure about his work, and that when the Buenos Aires creative team decided the old Man didn't work, he felt he'd screwed up. Seeing the play function so beautifully as he had written it reassured him; a nice gift for a small theater to be able to give a writer far from home.

That said, the fact that the play was successful in both forms affords some perspective on cultural differences as to the site of the "author". In the Anglo theater, for a director to simply cut a character that the writer will retain in the published play feels like an outrageous abuse of the writer. But in a theater whose authorial balance is tilted slightly more toward the director, it may feel like an appropriate distribution of artistic roles.

This notion holds true for many of these plays. Loza always publishes his full text, but the many productions of his work almost always trim some of the elaborations and repetitions that characterize his writing. The translations in this volume likewise render the texts in their entirety, but to follow the tradition in which they were written, performers of these translations might feel emboldened to impose edits.

Finally, an overarching note to potential performers of these works: the verse structure of Loza's plays might tempt English-language actors into slow, meditative performances—even potentially marking line breaks with breath. This would be very unlike the Argentine productions of these texts, which fly along in a great tumble of words.

PRODUCTION CREDITS

ORIGINAL SPANISH-LANGUAGE PRODUCTIONS[2]

Nada del amore me produce envidia

2008, Sportivo Teatral, Buenos Aires

Playwright	Santiago Loza
Performer	María Merlino
Costume design	Valentina Bari
Scenic design	Flor De Un Día
Lighting design	Fernanda Balcells
Events and tour production	Luz Algranti
Costume fabrication	Carmen Montecalvo
Fabric creation	Martín Sal
Music	Sandra Baylac
Graphic design	Florencia Bauza, Malena Castañon
Production assistant	Sonia Riobo
Wardrobe assistant	Liliana Piekar
Press	Carolina Alfonso
Producer	Flor De Un Día
Musical collaboration	Jape Ntaca
Director	Diego Lerman

2 All credits for original Spanish-language productions accessed at alternativateatral.com on September 10, 2021.

Pudor en animals de invierno

2011, Espacio Callejón, Buenos Aires

Playwright	Santiago Loza
Cast	Ricardo Félix, Valeria Roldán, Martin Shanly
Music	Lisandro Rodriguez
Costume design	Mariana Tirantte
Scenic design	Mariana Tirantte
Lighting design	Matías Sendón
Photography	Nora Lezano
Physical training	Leticia Mazur
Assistant director	Sofía Salvaggio
Press	María Sureda
Producer	María Sureda
Director	Lisandro Rodriguez

He nacido para verte sonreir

2011, Elefante Club de Teatro, Buenos Aires

Playwright	Santiago Loza
Cast	Luz Palazon, Martin Shanly
Costume design	Mariana Tirantte
Scenic design	Mariana Tirantte
Lighting design	Matías Sendón
Physical training	Leticia Mazur
Assistant director	Sofía Salvaggio
Press	María Sureda
Producers	Jose Escobar, Lisandro Rodriguez, María Sureda, Mariana Tirantte, Mariano Villamarin
Director	Lisandro Rodriguez

El mal de la montaña

2013, Abasto Social Club, Buenos Aires

Playwright	Santiago Loza
Cast	Patricio Aramburu, Pablo Cura, Julián Krakov, Natalia Señorales
Costume design	luz peña
Lighting design	Alejandro Le Roux
Sound design	Proyecto Gomez Casa
Photography	Sol Pittau
Assistant directors	Emanuel Parga, Sol Pittau
Press	Ana Garland
Director	Cristian Drut

La Mujer Puerca

2012, Elefante Club de Teatro, Buenos Aires

Playwright	Santiago Loza
Performer	Valeria Lois
Costume design	Jose Escobar, Lisandro Rodriguez
Scenic design	Jose Escobar, Lisandro Rodriguez
Lighting design	Matías Sendón
Photography	Nora Lezano
Graphic design	Lisandro Rodriguez
Assistant director	Cammila Gomez Grandoli
Press	María Sureda
Producers	Elefante Club De Teatro, Natalia Fernandez Acquier
Artistic collaborator	Mariano Villamarin
Director	Lisandro Rodriguez

ORIGINAL PRODUCTIONS OF TRANSLATIONS
COLLECTED IN THIS VOLUME

Winter Animals and *Nothing to Do with Love* [*Makes Me Envious*] were first produced in English in a double bill titled *Loza Plays* from April 25 to 29, 2017, in Ithaca, New York, by the Cherry Artists' Collective; Samuel Buggeln, Artistic Director.

CAST

Winter Animals

Son	Johnny Shea
Father	Dean Robinson*
Woman	Helen T Clark

Nothing to Do with Love [*Makes Me Envious*]

The Seamstress	Susannah Berryman*
	[*member, Actors' Equity Association]

CREATIVE TEAM

Original text	Santiago Loza
Translation	Samuel Buggeln and Ariel Gurevitch
Director, *Winter Animals*	Samuel Buggeln
Director, *Nothing to Do . . .*	Norman Johnson
Lighting	E. D. Intemann
Environments	Daniel Zimmerman
Sounds	Sergey Livitskiy
Costumes	Brock Viering
Production stage manager	Rachael Langton
Master electrician	Steven Blasberg
Assistant director	Kiefer Harrington
Environments associates	Aaron Roberts, Brock Viering
Lighting associate	Laura Dera
Run crew	Edith McCrea

CHERRY ARTS

Artistic director	Samuel Buggeln
Associate artistic director	Jennifer Herzog

SPECIAL THANKS

Community School of Music and Art, Cornell University Department of Performing and Media Arts, Ithaca College Department of Theater Arts, Sydney Hill, Craig MacDonald, Darcy Rose, David Studwell, Dave Williams.

The Saint was first produced in English as part of the *Listen to Her* festival from October 24 to November 3, 2019, at the Cherry Artspace in Ithaca, New York, by the Cherry Artists' Collective, Samuel Buggeln, Artistic Director.

CAST

The Girl	Jennifer Herzog*
The Man	Dean Robinson*
	[*member, Actors' Equity Association]

CREATIVE TEAM

Original text	Santiago Loza
Translation	Samuel Buggeln and Ariel Gurevitch
Director	Amina Omari
Lighting	Gabrielle Buttons
Stage manager	Ivy Stevens
Production assistants	Noah Elman, Francesca Infante-Meehan

CHERRY ARTS

Artistic director	Samuel Buggeln
Operations manager	Rose Howard
Marketing manager	Sarah Chaneles

SPECIAL THANKS

St. Luke's Church, Ithaca.